# JOSEPH MURUMBI

*A LEGACY OF INTEGRITY*

*KAREN ROTHMYER*

# JOSEPH MURUMBI
*A LEGACY OF INTEGRITY*

Copyright © 2018 by Karen Rothmyer

*Printed and bound in Kenya by*
**Colourprint Limited**

*Design & Layout by*
**Khalsa Lakhvir-Singh**

This book is sold subject to the condition that it shall not, by way of trade ot otherwise, be lent, resold, hired out, or otherwise circulated without the publisher's prior consent in any form of binding or cover other than that in which it is published and without a similar condition including this condition being imposed on the subsequent purchaser.

PUBLISHED BY
Zand Graphics

ISBN 978-9966-117-58-8

All illustrations that first appeared in *A Path Not Taken*
are used by permission of Alan Donovan.

*Joseph Murumbi in his library with a copy of Krapf's Kamba translation of 'The Gospel according to St. Mark'*

# JOSEPH MURUMBI
### A LEGACY OF INTEGRITY

## CONTENTS

6    *Preface*

9    *Introduction*

12   *Joseph Murumbi - a Chronology*

16   CHAPTER ONE
       **Becoming Murumbi**

42   CHAPTER TWO
       **Emergency and Exile**

84   CHAPTER THREE
       **The 'Reluctant Politician'**

147   CHAPTER FOUR
       **Art and the Search for Identity**

168   CHAPTER FIVE
       **The Later Years**

185   *Postscript*

189   *Acknowledgements*

191   *About the Author*

192   *Endnotes*

*A Nok terra cotta head, 500 B.C., as shown in an illustration in one of Murumbi's African art books.*

# JOSEPH MURUMBI
A LEGACY OF INTEGRITY

## PREFACE

Joseph Murumbi (1911-1990), Kenya's first Foreign Minister and second Vice-President, sat for a series of taped interviews in the late 1970s with a young doctoral researcher named Anne Thurston. She had become friendly with Murumbi and his wife Sheila in the course of using Murumbi's personal library at the couple's Nairobi home. At the time, Thurston says, Murumbi was keen on the idea of writing his autobiography, using the tapes as a starting point, and the two talked of cooperating in such an effort.

But Murumbi was slow to get going on the autobiography and that, combined with his health problems, ultimately doomed the project. Thurston edited some of the transcribed material from the tapes into three articles that appeared in *Kenya Past and Present*, a magazine put out by the Kenya Museum Society, but apart from that, the interviews remained out of the public eye. This continued for more than thirty years until Alan Donovan, Murumbi's partner in the African Heritage gallery in Nairobi, pulled them together with some other material, most notably an interview Murumbi had done with John Platter of United Press International, and arranged for them to be published in 2015 as a book titled *A Path Not Taken: The Story of Joseph Murumbi*. This was done under the auspices of the Murumbi Trust, an entity Donovan had founded.

## Preface

The Murumbi interviews represent one of the few acutely observed, personal accounts of Kenya's independence-era politics. As such, they are of value not only to historical researchers of the future but also to individual Kenyans, especially younger Kenyans, who want to know more about how their country came to be.

After reading *A Path Not Taken* shortly after it was published, my friend Wendy Karmali and I—both of whom had lived in Kenya through portions of the Murumbi years—agreed that the interviews were fascinating. But in order to appeal to a wide audience, they needed to be significantly edited and provided with context.

We approached Donovan and Thurston and got their agreement to our taking on the project. Unfortunately, Wendy had to withdraw from the project soon thereafter owing to family health problems.

The Thurston interviews of Murumbi contained in this book have been re-organized, in some cases quite radically, and occasionally Murumbi's wording has been slightly altered to clarify meaning. The interviews have been combined with material from the original Thurston transcripts that was not included in *A Path Not Taken*, as well as with other interviews such as those recorded by Platter.

The introductions to the various sections attempt to fill in useful facts and background information. They also add the voices of people who interacted with Murumbi or who are experts on aspects of his life or times. The quotes from Murumbi in these sections are all from *A Path Not Taken* or from the original transcripts.

For the most part I have footnoted only directly quoted material from books, archives, etc., or from the interviews I did, on the grounds that this book is meant to be what might be termed an enhanced memoir, not an academic treatise. I have corrected, where I could, any minor mistakes in dates and similar items in the original transcripts, while avoiding, I hope, the introduction of any new errors.

Any net proceeds from this book will go to furthering the work of the Murumbi Trust.

*Karen Rothmyer*
*2018*

*Mask of a Benin King, an illustration in one of Murumbi's African art books*

INTRODUCTION

# A 'Role Model' of a Good Kenyan

Joseph Zuzarte Murumbi was remarkable for several reasons, starting with the fact that as a young man he rejected the widespread tradition of being identified as belonging to his father's community—in this case Goans from a Portuguese colony on India's west coast—and instead fought successfully to be officially registered as part of his mother's community, the Maasai. Even then, he was hardly a typical Maasai: he did all of his schooling in English-speaking schools in India, and never became fluent in the Maasai language.

Yet in independence-era Kenya, this unusual background didn't prevent Murumbi from rising to the top of the country's political leadership. That is partly a tribute to Murumbi's own character and talent. But it also says something important about how, in those years, a devotion to building the nation could, and often did, take precedence over ethnic loyalties.

Another remarkable thing about Murumbi is that his political career came late in life and lasted a relatively short time. Following his schooling in India, he lived for a few years in Kenya and then for approximately a decade in Somalia, where he worked as an employee of the

British Military and as a small businessman. At the age of 41 he returned to Kenya and joined the Kenya African Union just months before the imposition of a State of Emergency in late 1952. Nine years of exile followed shortly thereafter, at the end of which he came home and was elected to Parliament in 1963. He became Foreign Minister in independent Kenya's first Government and in mid-1966 President Jomo Kenyatta named him Vice-President. But by the end of that year he had resigned, and never again in the remaining quarter-century of his life did he engage in active politics. Instead, until ill-health intervened, he devoted himself to his art collection, to private business, and, later, to his farm in Maasailand.

How did Murumbi accomplish so much in public life in such a short time? Luck played a role: as one example, he was named to the leadership of the KAU in 1952 only because all the sitting leaders had been arrested. But he also made the most of the opportunities that came his way: Kenyatta was so impressed by Murumbi's competence during the 1962 independence talks in London that he made him, in effect, his private secretary. And after Murumbi proved his value in everything from raising campaign funds to persuading Maasai leaders to back Kenyatta's party, Kenyatta appointed him to top jobs in his Government.

Throughout his time in high office, Murumbi remained modest and unassuming. 'When I became Vice-President, I refused to have a police escort, which the Vice-President is entitled to,' he recalled later. 'What interested me was to do my job and do my job honestly, and to serve my country faithfully.'

And when he felt he could no longer do that, he resigned.

What comes across in talking with people who knew Murumbi is that he was, above all, a decent and honourable human being. He was not a towering political figure like Kenyatta, or a towering intellect like Tom Mboya. Histories of the period do not attach his name to any significant political event or accord. Rather, he is important to Kenya's history as a man who played his part, and played it well. As Professor Godfrey Muriuki, a leading Kenyan historian, puts it, Murumbi was 'a role model of what a good Kenyan should be'.

Viewed in the context of the independence era in which ideological and political battles over how to develop the country were being fought out, and in which the corruption that was later to reach epidemic proportions was only beginning to take hold, Murumbi stands as a reminder of how Kenya's history might have been different. But just as important, Murumbi is an example of the ability of human beings, no matter what their background or the era into which they are born, to lead full lives and to contribute in important ways to making their country, and the world, a better place.

# JOSEPH MURUMBI
### A LEGACY OF INTEGRITY

## CHRONOLOGY

**1911**
Born on 18 June in Eldama Ravine, Kenya, the only child of Peter Zuzarte, a Goan, and the grand-daughter of Murumbi, a Maasai leader. He is christened Joseph Anthony Zuzarte.

**1918**
Goes to India at the age of about 7, where he studies at a Catholic primary school and later at a Catholic secondary school in the town of Bellary. After secondary school he works as a clerk.

**1933**
Returns to Kenya. Chooses to take on legal status as a Maasai and is given land by the community near Nakuru. Works with his father growing vegetables for sale.

**1935**
Goes to Nairobi after his father's death and gets a job as a clerk in a Government hospital.

**1941**
Goes to Somalia with the British Military Administration. Spends most of the next several years there working

as a clerk and administrator. Also engages in two unsuccessful business ventures. Marries a Somali woman named Cecilia and they have one son.

**1952**
Returns to Kenya and gets a job with a transport company. Joins the Kenya African Union, meets Pio Gama Pinto and Jomo Kenyatta. Becomes known as Joseph Zuzarte Murumbi. Named acting KAU secretary.

**1952-1953**
Assists with the defence of Kenyatta and his colleagues at the Kapenguria trial.

**1953**
Leaves Kenya, at Kenyatta's request, in March, after being instructed to tell the world about the Kenya freedom struggle. Shortly after he leaves, the KAU is banned, meaning he will be arrested if he returns to Kenya. He travels to India, Egypt and England, where he spends the next nine years in exile.

**1954**
Becomes Assistant Secretary of the Movement for Colonial Freedom. In this capacity he travels widely, both within Britain and beyond.

**1957**
Becomes a press aide at the Moroccan Embassy and is encouraged by the Moroccans to also continue his political work. As a side business, he buys and sells African books, and he starts collecting art. During these years he meets Sheila Kaine, who is to become his second wife.

**1960-1963**
Assists African delegates at a succession of Lancaster House talks on Kenyan independence. Acts as an aide to Kenyatta at the 1962 talks, at the end of which Kenyatta asks him to come to Kenya and work for him.

**1962**
Returns to Nairobi and immediately begins reorganizing Kenyatta's office and the headquarters of the Kenya African National Union, in preparation for the upcoming elections.

**1963**
Wins a seat as a KANU Member of Parliament for Nairobi South in the May pre-independence elections.

**1963**
Named Minister of State for Foreign Affairs.

**1963**
In office when Kenya becomes independent in December.

**1964**
Appointed Foreign Minister.

**1966**
Named Vice-President in May, 1966, replacing Jaramogi Oginga Odinga. Shortly thereafter, with Kenyatta's agreement, he accepts a job as chairman of a new Kenyan subsidiary of Rothmans International, a tobacco company, but continues for the rest of the year to represent Kenya at key meetings.

**1966**
Leaves Government in December.

**Late 1960s**
After Rothmans closes down its Kenyan subsidiary, he takes board seats on several companies including Bamburi Cement and Kenya Construction Co.

**1973**
Starts African Heritage in 1973 in partnership with Alan Donovan. The company runs a gallery in Nairobi and showcases African art and fashion around the world.

**1977**
Given land by the Maasai in Trans Mara and builds a house there, with plans to raise cattle and engage in other farming ventures.

**1982**
Returns to Nairobi, after a fall and increasing ill-health.

**1990**
Dies on 21 June, and is buried in Nairobi's City Park close to Pio Gama Pinto. His wife Sheila is later laid to rest alongside him in 2000 in what is now the Murumbi Peace Memorial Garden.

CHAPTER ONE

# *Becoming Murumbi*

The person now remembered as Joseph Murumbi, Kenya's second Vice-President and one of Africa's most famous art collectors, only emerged from the wings of history after many years during which he was known as Joseph Anthony Zuzarte. From his birth in Eldama Ravine in 1911 through his schooling in India, and then through several years back in Kenya followed by roughly ten years in Somalia, he was forming the interests and personality that would be evident later on. But during all of those years, he very likely seemed to the world at large to be simply another person leading a fairly conventional life.

Exactly when Joseph Anthony Zuzarte became Joseph Murumbi is somewhat unclear. By implication Murumbi suggests it occurred in his twenties when he first got land in Maasailand, thanks to his Maasai mother, and won his fight to be classified as a Maasai. But according to Fitz de Souza, a Goan Kenyan lawyer who helped with Jomo Kenyatta's defence trial and later served as Deputy Speaker of Parliament, he was still going by his father's name, Zuzarte, at least fifteen years later.[1] It's possible that for some considerable period Murumbi used both names as it suited him. But one thing seems indisputable: it was only when he returned to Kenya from Somalia, more than four decades after his birth, that the life of the man the world would come to know as Joseph Murumbi truly began.

*Joseph Murumbi as a small boy*

*Joseph Murumbi's mother*

*Peter Zuzarte - Joseph Murumbi's father*

*Joseph Murumbi's grandfather*

*Becoming Murumbi*

## The Formation of Character

By Murumbi's own account, two of the most important influences on him during his school years in southern India were Mother Elizabeth, who treated him with special affection, and Father Callenberg, who helped everyone regardless of religion or race.

Later, after he returned as a young adult to Kenya, the two years he spent with his own father reinforced Father Callenberg's teachings. Like Callenberg, his father seems never to have turned down a request for help, and to have made friends far and wide—from a British game warden at Eldama Ravine to fellow Asian traders. (According to Murumbi, it was the game warden's wife who persuaded his mother to let him go for schooling to India).

Speaking about Murumbi as they knew him in his later life, acquaintances invariably refer to Murumbi's kindness to poor people and the ease with which he made friends across all levels of society. 'As soon as people knew him they warmed to him,' recalls Alan Donovan, his later business partner. 'He was always noted for his fairness. He believed in the equality of all people.' [2]

Another aspect of Murumbi's personality that developed in India was an aversion to racial discrimination, along with a self-confidence unaffected by British colonial attitudes. Murumbi doesn't refer in his reminiscences to any personal encounters with discrimination while at school, and in fact, in an outline for his proposed autobiography, he says that while he at first appeared to his classmates at Bellary 'as an oddity', within a short time he was fully accepted. But he describes in strong terms his distress at hearing the mostly Anglo-Indian students at his school—Anglo-Indians being those who were a mix of English and Indian heritage—refer to full Indians as 'niggers'.

Was Murumbi, who served in the prestigious post of school prefect, regarded as a sort of 'honorary' Anglo-Indian? Murumbi doesn't say. But his mostly cheerful account of his school years suggests that whatever the case, his Goan-Maasai heritage appears not to have been a major issue.

Once he returned as a young adult to Kenya, he would have become aware that serious relationships and marriages between Asians like his father and Africans like his mother, while not common, weren't all that unusual in the colony's early years. Muzzafar Khan, whose mother was the half-Maasai second wife of one such Asian—the first wife was a full Maasai—says in an account published in *Settling in a Strange Land: Stories of Punjabi Muslim Pioneers in Kenya* that he knew 'at least 25 or 30 mixed families in the old days'. (He himself was born in 1941.) 'I have never had any problem about being of mixed parentage...I don't have any complex,' he said.[3]

There were a sufficient number of such families that around 1958, according to the editor of the book, a group of young Asian-Africans in Nairobi formed a short-lived association and named Murumbi as their patron.[4]

Murumbi's mixed heritage never seems to have been an issue for him politically. 'Being half-Maasai and half-Goan meant he would be acceptable to both Luos and Kikuyus,' says Professor Godfrey Muriuki. 'The Maasai were no threat.'[5]

One fact worth remembering in this regard is that Kenyan Africans in the early independence era were much less ethnically divided than they would later become. As Charles Hornsby notes in his monumental *Kenya: A History Since Independence*, in the elections of May 1963 in which Murumbi was elected to Parliament from a mixed racial constituency, 'half-Maasai John Keen [his father was German] stood in Luhya-dominated Trans-Nzoia, and KANU's candidates in three of four Nakuru district seats, dominated by Kalenjin and Kikuyu, were Luo or Luhya.' In that same election, there were five Asians and only three Kikuyus out of twenty-five candidates in heavily Kikuyu-populated Nairobi.[6]

Even as Murumbi's personality was developing at Bellary, so, too, were his very considerable skills. Starting with his rigorous Jesuit training and first job as a clerk, Murumbi showed a level of natural talent, no doubt combined with hard work and a reputation for honesty, which a quarter-century later led to his becoming the highly-paid Deputy Controller of Imports and Exports in the British Military Administration in Somalia.

It didn't take Jomo Kenyatta long to recognize Murumbi's abilities. During the second Lancaster House talks that led to independence, Murumbi, who at that time was still in exile in London, served as an aide to Kenyatta, typing his correspondence and arranging meetings. Just before Kenyatta left for Nairobi, according to Murumbi's recollections, he asked Murumbi to come to work for him in Nairobi. And after independence, Murumbi was given increasing responsibilities.

One final aspect of Murumbi's years in India that is worth considering briefly is the way his education shaped his world view. In India, as in all the colonies, the subjects he studied, and the ideological framework within which they were taught, were British. He cared deeply about poor people and hated racism, but this didn't lead him to Karl Marx or Frantz Fanon. Instead, during his exile in London he joined the British Labour Party, and he later listed his hobbies as including stamp collecting and gardening.

*Family Matters*

While Murumbi was, by all accounts, a remarkably moral and decent person, there were inevitably some aspects of his personality that were less attractive. The most troubling is Murumbi's rejection of Cecilia, his first wife, who, according to De Souza, he met in Somalia, and their son George, known as JoJo, his only known offspring.[7] A restricted file in the Kenya National Archives is described as containing Murumbi's marriage certificate dated May 29, 1944, but the certificate itself is missing.

When Murumbi returned from England in 1962 with a British woman, Sheila Kaine, whom he subsequently married in a traditional Maasai ceremony, he appears to have pushed Cecilia and his son completely out of his life. De Souza, who knew the Murumbi family quite well, recalled in a 2014 interview that 'Cecilia signed documents that she was willing to get a divorce and Joe arranged for me to pay her a monthly sum when she went back to Somalia...We do not know what happened to her or the child.'[8]

Muthoni Likimani, a Kenyan author and broadcaster whose husband was the Murumbis' family doctor, says there may have been reasons for the break-up beyond Sheila's arrival on the scene. During Murumbi's years in exile, she says, Cecilia began living with another man, a

Somali, and had children with him. She recalls Cecilia as quiet, with what appeared to be a relatively low level of education, able to speak Kiswahili but not English. Sheila, by contrast, was a librarian and lover of books.

Still, how to account for the heartlessness Murumbi displayed? Before Cecilia left for Somalia, De Souza recalled, 'she gave me some books as she had no money, she depended on us for food. Eventually Joe and Sheila claimed those books and took them away.'⁹ Similarly, Emma Pinto, the widow of Murumbi's close friend Pio Gama Pinto, told Benegal Pereira, a Kenyan of Goan descent now living in America, that JoJo used to come to the Murumbi's house occasionally to ask for sweets and money. 'Sheila used to chase him away,' Pereira quotes her as saying.¹⁰

Possibly the only explanation for Murumbi's behaviour, which included a total unwillingness to discuss his family, is his complete devotion to Sheila. 'Sheila was uncomfortable' about Murumbi's prior relationship, according to Anne Thurston. And to Murumbi, she says, 'Sheila was more important than anything'. She describes the couple as so close as to be 'their own complete world'.¹¹

## The Power of Books

Murumbi, by his own admission, knew little about the independence movement in India while he was living there, or about Kenya's independence movement when he first returned home. He dates his political awakening to two books his father gave him at that time.

The first, *India in Bondage*, was written by Jabez T Sunderland, a clergyman whose family had emigrated from Britain to America when he was a child. As Sunderland explains in the book, before making two trips to India in the 1890s and in 1913-14 he had read only British accounts of

India. Upon visiting India, however, he realized these accounts had completely misrepresented the country.

The titles of some of the chapters of the book, first published in 1929, give a flavour of the outrage he felt on India's behalf: 'The great delusion: Britain's claim that she is "educating India for self-rule"'; 'The great farce: Britain's claim that India is her "sacred trust"'.

Throughout, Sunderland's tone is white-hot fury, but the strength of the book lies in the pages and pages of facts and figures, along with lists of India's achievements and numerous quotes from Englishmen critical of British colonial behaviour. A veteran who served in America's Civil War, Sunderland claims that at least one-third of Indians 'are actually worst housed, worst clothed and worst fed than the slaves of America' ever were. [12]

According to the Unitarian-Universalist Association (Sunderland became a Unitarian after leaving the Baptist denomination), *Time* magazine praised Sunderland's arguments, while Mohandas Gandhi and poet Rabindranath Tagore both sent him letters of gratitude. The book, however, was banned by the British colonial Government in India. [13]

By the time Murumbi was reading this book, the struggle for Indian independence was well underway, and because of the large Indian population in Kenya, some of that movement's ideas and fervour spilled over into Kenya. As one example, Benegal Pereira says that his father, Eddie Pereira, was fined repeatedly by the Kenya colonial Government for supporting Indian independence. [14]

Asian Kenyans were generally supportive of the early Kenyan independence struggle. In 1923, Asians fought against the white settlers' efforts to impose restrictions on Indian immigration and land ownership, enlisting Africans in their effort. The result was a halt to the settlers' march toward a whites-only Government. The British Colonial Office issued a White Paper known as the Devonshire Declaration —remarkable in its sentiment though hardly an accurate description of policy going forward—that while the rights of all groups in Kenya must be safeguarded, 'the interests of the African natives must be paramount'. Asians' attitude toward the African struggle remained relatively sympathetic until the British colonial Governor imposed a State of Emergency in 1952, at which time an increasing number of Asians concluded they were safer under British rule; even then, however, some continued, often covertly, to support the independence cause. Notable among the Asians who spoke out publicly was Makhan Singh, a trade unionist who shared detention with Kenyatta, only to be side-lined after independence.

The second book, *Kenya from Within: A Short Political History*, published in 1927, was written by W McGregor Ross, a British civil engineer who served in various posts including director of public works for the Kenya protectorate/colony and as a member of the Kenya Legislature.

Ross is remarkably candid in the book about what he regards as the injustices done by the colonial settlers. As one example, he disputes the virtually uniformly-held European contention that there were immense areas of unoccupied land in Kenya when the Europeans arrived. Instead, he argues that some of these areas were a no man's land between hostile tribes, some had inferior soil or other natural problems, and some belonged to the pastoralist Maasai who were so feared that even if they weren't always around other tribes didn't trespass. [15]

The British takeover of the interior only succeeded, he says, because the local people weren't sophisticated enough to realize what was going on—a condition that allowed for 'so many of the exploits of the Foreign Office which have been regarded as brilliant.' [16] Thus, the Kikuyu became squatters and the Maasai were forced into ever smaller and less desirable territory.

Ross also foresaw the kind of society which settler-dominated Kenya was fast becoming. He writes that white young people were growing up as 'a type which no Empire need be proud of: domineering, repellent in its self-glorification, little-minded'.[17] Ross's concerns about settler society proved well-founded. By the time Murumbi was reading his book a few years after its publication, British settlers in Kenya had created a race-determined political and social system that closely resembled those of Rhodesia and South Africa.

Nor was it only Kenya's white settlers who harboured racist sentiments; racism was also common among Britain's colonial administrators. Even Malcolm MacDonald, the last British Governor of Kenya, with whom Murumbi was always on friendly terms, wrote of Kenyan leaders on the eve of independence: 'Not far behind their masks of modern nationalist politicians lurk the grimaces of their inherited tribal faces, expressing all the mutual rivalries, suspicions, antagonisms and primitive instincts which prevailed in Kenya up to a few decades ago, and which might still run amok once more.' [18]

*Becoming Murumbi*

## The Story of a Grandfather

Murumbi says very little in his reminiscences about his Maasai relatives, but one of whom he is clearly very proud is his mother's father, a well-known leader (or laibon) of the Uasin Gishu Maasai. A brief mention of him is made in *Early Days in East Africa* by Sir Frederick Jackson, Lieutenant-Governor for the East Africa protectorate between 1907 and 1911.

Murumbi, in his reminiscences, makes some disparaging comments about Jackson, seeming to confuse what Jackson said about Murumbi's grandfather (here spelled Mirumbi) with what he said about another leader. While Jackson was certainly not a particularly sympathetic chronicler, his account is nevertheless of interest, if only because of its rarity:

'When I arrived at the Ravine to take over [as head of the province] the lybon of southern Kamassia, a one-eyed man, came to see me, and was introduced as a very useful man, and for a few months he proved himself to be so,' Jackson writes. 'But he was not a Kamassia at all; he was a Uasin Gishu Maasai, and, true to type, he soon began to stir up trouble. It first started through his followers, one small lot after another, leaving him, and joining Mirumbi.

'...[O]ne night he sent a raiding party to attack Mirumbi's one manyatta at the foot of the hill just below the station. It occurred about 2 a.m. in bright moonlight, and was so well and expeditiously carried out that, in a matter of a few minutes, they had killed two *moran* of Mirumbi's cattle guard, lost two of their own, set fire to all the huts, except Mirumbi's which was enclosed in a small stockade, and got away with all his cattle, some forty-odd head.' [19]

IN MURUMBI'S WORDS

# Becoming Murumbi

My father, Peter Zuzarte, was from an old landed Goan family who lived in a place called Giri, in Goa. They were quite a well-to-do family, with their own chapel and priest. My father, however, wanted to go abroad, and when he heard that clerks were being hired for work in East Africa, he applied for a job and was selected to come, arriving in 1897. He then walked to Baringo Station where he served as a district clerk. Later, he was posted to Naivasha and from there he went to Eldama Ravine.

In Eldama Ravine he gave up his job and started his own shop. It was there that he met my mother, and it was there that I was born, in 1911. Later we moved to Londiani, where he again set up a shop.

My mother grew up in the Eldama Ravine area. She was the daughter of Murumbi, the laibon of the Uasin Gishu Maasai. On one occasion my grandfather incited the Maasai warriors and the Sudanese, who had been stationed at Eldama Ravine by Lord Lugard, to rebel against the British. They nearly killed the District Commissioner. My grandfather was deported to Narok then and on two other occasions. The third time he died there.

My father's shop in Londiani was situated in an area away from the main Indian trading area. It was a corrugated iron building, rather a big shop, and our residence was attached at one end;

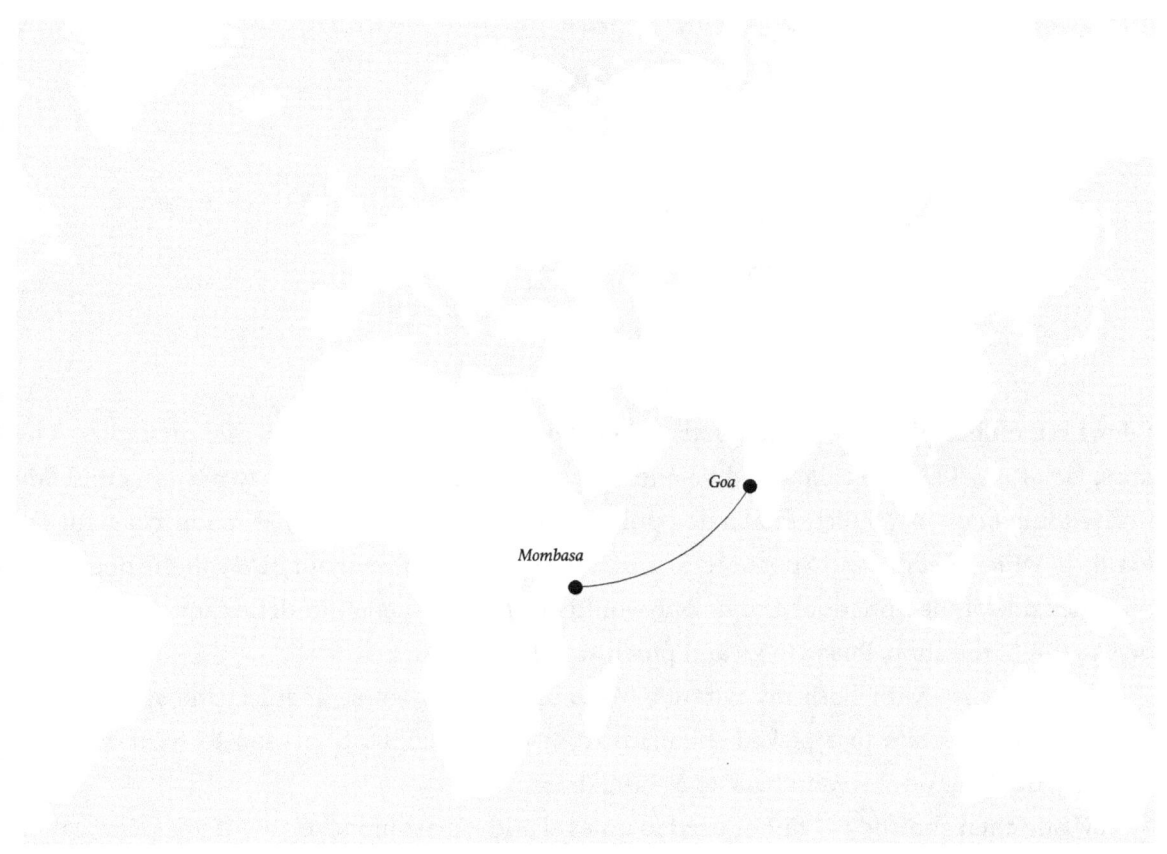

behind was a kitchen. It was the only shop in the area where one could buy drinks and a good range of supplies. I remember as a child seeing the Boer settlers, arriving in wagons pulled by teams of oxen, stop at my father's shop. After Londiani, where there was a railhead, there was no other real source of supplies until Kitale or Eldoret. When there weren't many customers, I would sit in the shop with my father and he would teach me the alphabet.

My father used to grow roses and he told me, although I don't remember the incident, that Teddy Roosevelt once came to Londiani and, my father's shop being the only place where he could buy supplies, he called there and saw the roses. He and my father exchanged information about grafting them.

My father used to go out every morning, practicing shooting in the Londiani forest. He used to shoot green pigeons and bring them home for dinner. He often wrote petitions and letters for people. He always kept contact with his friends and they kept contact with him.

## Roddie, Spot and roasted ribs

I don't remember playing with anybody other than our dogs, my mother, and my father. The dogs, Jack Russells, were called Roddie and Spot and were very important to me as a child. My first reading book had a picture of a dog pulling a little cart, and my father made a cart for me to ride in which Roddie and Spot used to pull. When my father went out he'd call the dogs to sit on either side of the front door and no one would be allowed to enter until he came back. When he was out of the shop, I used to go and pinch sugar and eat it.

I spoke English with both my parents. My mother was a great linguist. She spoke about eleven languages; she just picked them up from other people. She used to wear Western clothing, but later on she went back to Maasai dress.

Now and then she and my father used to quarrel and she would take me off to a place called Kedawa, which is very close to Londiani, where she had friends. I remember riding strapped to her back; I still remember its warmth and how I used to fall asleep. I remember, too, going through the Londiani forest and being impressed by some little red birds there. Eventually there would be a reconciliation and then she'd come back.

At Kedawa there was a big Nandi and Maasai population and they held feasts there. I remember all the old people sitting down in a circle, in the centre of which was a big pot which contained a brew. Each man had a long reed which he dipped in the pot to suck the brew. When they slaughtered a bull or other animal, all had a good feast and my mother used to give me roasted ribs. I'd sit there with my roasted rib, tugging at it and enjoying it very much.

It was very cold in Londiani and I used to sleep in front of the fireplace. Before I went to sleep my mother always brought me a cup of beaten egg, what they call zabaglione in Italian. It's egg white beaten up with some milk, brandy and sugar—eggnog. Then my mother used to kiss me good night and lift my legs up and tuck the blankets under my feet.

I lived in Londiani until I was about six or seven years old. Then my father decided I should be educated in India. At first my mother was very, very angry and she took me away to Kedawa. My father then sent a friend of my mother's to explain why it would benefit me to go to India, and finally my mother relented and let me go. I was not to see her again for many years.

I remember particularly a suit I had made for me before I went. It was a sort of greenish woollen suit with braces and a belt, and it had a big collar with a black bow. The trousers were short and narrow and came below the knee, with buttons at the bottom, and I wore long socks. I had a tweed cap, too. My father had a wooden box made for me and let me choose the colour it was painted—chocolate-red like the water tanks at the railway station near the house.

I don't remember the train journey from Londiani, but I remember going to Mombasa and travelling to Bombay on a ship. It was very hot on the ship because ships were coal-fired in those days. We landed at Bombay and stayed there for a week or two, and then my father took me to Mysore in south India. From there we went to Bangalore.

## India: The Jesuits and Charlie Chaplin

My father had arranged with the nuns of the school I was going to go to that he would bring me. We sat in the parlour and he spoke to the nuns. Suddenly I realized that he had left, and I ran to find him. Of course I was brought back again. The nuns gave me a cricket bat to try to divert me, and in time I settled down at the school.

It was a very good school, run by Jesuits. They ran the school very much on the lines of an English public school with an emphasis on leadership and sports. Most of the students were Anglo-Indian, but there were a few European boys as well.

When I was about 12 I moved to a school in Bellary, another town in south India, also run by

Jesuits. Discipline was humanitarian, but it was very tough, and sometimes we resented it. However, afterwards I realized that being subjected to discipline and to religious teachings gave me an anchor in life, a conscience with which to judge what is wrong and try to do what is right. Much of my character and many of my values were formed at Bellary.

The majority of the students were Anglo-Indians, half-Indian and half-European. They ranged in colour from coal-black to pure white, but they used to call the Indians niggers and that used to annoy me very much. I told them, 'You people forget your background: your mothers were Indian and your fathers were Europeans, although you may be from one or two generations later, and you're Indians and not something different.' But they were encouraged to feel different by the colonial Government: an Anglo-Indian could find a secure job in the Post and Telegraphs, the railways, the customs, or the police, because these jobs were reserved for Anglo-Indians.

I was a prefect at the school and I learned that you had a certain amount of power over people but it wasn't right to take advantage of people in trouble. Whenever somebody did something wrong, I tried to find out why he did it. If someone stole a pencil, for instance, he probably couldn't afford a pencil. So rather than jump to conclusions and punish a person, you must find out the reasons why he has done something wrong, and if you find out the reasons, you must try to help him to avoid doing this again. Power is something which you can abuse and something which you can use in the right manner, and be of help to people. In later life you have people working under you and you are responsible for them and you've got to temper your treatment of people with justice, and that's where I learned it. And it's served me throughout my life.

There were two people at the school who were tremendously important to me. Mother Elizabeth was a Portuguese nun, about thirty-five years old. She loved me very much and she looked after me like her own child. It was she who gave me my first pair of long trousers. You see, I had to cling to something, I didn't know whether my mother was alive or dead, and she helped me to fill the gap. I worshipped her as a boy. I remember following her everywhere she went.

Some people used to donate things to the school like old shoes and ties. I got a pair of shoes that I liked very much—I liked pointed shoes—although they were too big for me. I told Mother that I must have those shoes so she said, 'Here you are, have them.' I used to stuff them with cotton to make them so they would fit me, but I was very much Charlie Chaplin.

The other person was the principal, Father Callenberg. He was loved by people of all religious communities in Bellary because he never showed any discrimination between Catholics and Protestants, Hindus or Muslims. Whenever a poor man came to him he helped him, no matter what his religion was.

When I was two years from finishing my secondary education, my father's shop burned down and he had no money to pay for my education. I didn't know what was going to happen to me, but Father Callenberg took over paying for my education, and I was able to complete it. Later, when I was working in Bellary, I did what I could to make a contribution to the school in gratitude for what Father Callenberg had done. Without his help I don't know what would have happened to me.

There is another reason I shall never forget Father Callenberg. From the age of seven until I left school at the age of nineteen, I was cloistered between the four walls of a school; I had hardly any experience with the outside world. When I finished school, I found the world outside a complete contradiction to what I had been used to and I got so confused that I lost my faith.

When Father Callenberg noticed that I was not coming to church, he asked me why, and in response I wrote him a long letter telling him how confused I was. We carried on a correspondence for about two years, and in the end he brought me back to the belief that God did exist and was all powerful. I'm not very religious in the sense of going to church every Sunday, but I have maintained this firm belief in the power of God.

Sometimes, when I've been in some trouble, I've got up in the middle of the night and knelt down and prayed to God, and invariably, God has helped me. I've found the solution to my problem, or somebody has come whom I didn't know, or a person I've spoken to has come forth and helped me. And I've seen this happen to me and my father, who helped many other people.

## The World Grows Bigger

Father Callenberg helped me to get a job as a clerk after I finished school, first in a garage and later in a company called Burmah Shell. I lived with an extremely nice family called the O'Malleys. Old man O'Malley was an Anglo-Indian, and his wife was an Indian. Just as Mother Elizabeth had, Mrs O'Malley looked after me like a mother. Moreover, she was one of the best cooks in the world and she encouraged me to learn to cook. If I had stayed on, I might have become a depot superintendent. But my boss, Mr O'Connor, was sacked, so I resigned.

When I left Burmah Shell I got a job doing famine relief work in the villages in south India, keeping the muster roles and helping to plot the roads. The people in the villages were terribly kind and honest. It was in the villages that I first had contact with the caste system. I didn't really understand the system at all, but when I shook hands with the lower caste Hindus or brought them water from a well, I was told by the higher caste Hindus that this was wrong. This was the beginning of my political conscience.

When the famine relief work was over, after about nine months, I got a job in an ice factory making ice. When the slack season came, my boss sent me to the workshop. One Sunday morning I was waiting for my relief when I saw young O'Malley coming toward me with an elderly man. I thought the man had come to buy some ice and asked what I could do for him. He looked at me with a painful expression and said, 'I don't think you'll remember me. I left here many years ago.' Something instinctively told me that it was my father. When my relief came I went with my father to the railway station, because he had to catch a train.

My first question to my father was: 'Where is my mother?' He and my mother had separated but he said he would write to me about her, and not long afterward he wrote asking me if I could come back to Kenya as he was in difficulty and needed my help. My father and my stepmother [a woman named Mrs Ezalda Dias, previously married to a clerk working in Kenya] had quarrelled and he was thrown out of the house and I think he had all of his property in her name and was left penniless. When he returned to Kenya he made enquiries about my mother, and he wrote again to tell me that she had been killed by a lion. When I heard this, I answered that I didn't think I'd come back. My father then made further enquiries and wrote to me and told me that he had made a mistake, that she was alive, and that she wanted me to come.

## Home to Kenya

At this time, in 1931, my father was living in Nakuru where two Indians were helping him, and I think they probably gave him the money to bring me from India. When I met my father in Nakuru, I asked if I could see my mother. He said, 'Don't worry, tomorrow I'm sending you by car to a place called Njoro, and you'll meet your mother.' The next morning when I arrived at Njoro, my mother wasn't there. She had gone to the railway station as she thought I was coming by train. However, there were many old Maasai women who knew I was my mother's child and they were all so happy to see me. I was kissed by all the old ladies and somebody ran to the station to tell my mother that I had arrived.

Presently I saw a group of women coming, about twenty of them, and I said to myself, 'Oh no, which of these is my mother?' As they approached me, one of them detached herself and came running, and I thought she must be my mother. And she was absolutely crazy when she saw me. She wept and said, 'God, my God, thank you, thank you.' And that night when I was going to bed, she sat on my bed, talking to me, and she lifted the end of my feet and tucked the blanket underneath. And I cried. She asked me, 'Why are you crying?' I said, 'Mummy, I still remember when I was a baby you used to tuck my blanket underneath.'

My father and I discussed the possibilities of what I might do, and I think his advice was very sound. He said, 'Now, my son, you have come back and I can get you a good job. But I don't want you to get a job. I want you to get some land in Maasai, identify yourself with the Maasai, your mother's people. You are educated and they need you more than my people, the Asians.' He said that when I had made some money I should go to England, study law, and come back and help my people.

I had a big struggle to get the Government to recognize me as an African. When I applied for land, the Government officials were very suspicious. The Provincial Commissioner, Mr Hodge, said, 'Look here, you're not a Maasai, you're an Asian.' And in that respect he was right; one takes the nationality of one's father. I said, 'That's true, but I don't want to be known as an Asian. I'm willing to renounce my Asian nationality.' Then he referred my case to the Attorney-General, and the Attorney-General ruled that I had the option either to stick to my Asian nationality and give up any rights as an African, or vice-versa.

I went back to Hodge and said that I wanted to be considered an African, and I signed a declaration to say that I had no claim at all to any rights and privileges of the Asian community. I've never changed in this decision or regretted it.

## Life in Kampi Moto

Then the question was where I wanted land. I selected a spot in an area called Kampi Moto, near my mother's people, though my mother didn't live there; she lived in Mau Narok. I applied for the land and my application had to be approved by the chiefs and elders. They kept haggling over it, and finally the District Officer of Baringo called a *baraza* at Eldama Ravine which I was asked to attend.

When I said I wanted land, the chiefs and elders first refused. Then I asked them whether my mother had rights to land as a Maasai. They said, 'Your mother has every right to the land, she can have land anywhere.' I said, 'All right, my mother will make an application.' They couldn't raise objection to that, and in the end they had to give way. I got the land directly in my name.

My father came with me to the land and he had a little market garden, about five acres of the twenty I had. We used to sell our vegetables in Nakuru, which was about twenty-five miles away. We lived there for about two years. We stayed in a tent because we didn't dare risk building a house as the place was so full of termites.

I became very interested in the game that came to our land. There was for instance an ostrich, he usually came every second day to the river and drank water and then went away. I used to put a handful of maize just near the river on his path to the river. Well, he saw the maize and he gobbled it up. And then I used to put this maize further and further away from the river and close to our tents. Eventually he had a habit of coming, drinking his water and coming up near our tents and eating his maize and going away and he wasn't frightened at all. It just shows you that animals have a natural fear but if you can overcome that fear they can be approachable, they can be friendly in a sense.

Later, when I was in Nairobi, I bought a baby ram and I brought him up on a feeding bottle. I also had a Persian cat and a dog. And we used to go out for a walk in the evening, all three of us, and the dog, even when he was a puppy without any training, used to keep us all together.

## Political Awakening

My father gave me two books which influenced my political thinking. The first book I read was *India in Bondage*, which opened my eyes to what the British rule in India was like and how people were suffering, and how they were struggling, and what their hopes were to be free men. And then I read *Kenya from Within* by McGregor Ross. One could see the same pattern of colonial exploitation. I wasn't politically motivated yet but it made me think that in Kenya we had a situation, in India we had a situation, where people were being exploited by a colonial power. And exploitation is wrong.

These two books influenced me considerably and I began to take an interest in and learn more about Kenya politics. When I came to realize what was happening in Kenya, I was shocked and horrified. And that made me conscious of the politics of the country. But I didn't take any steps toward entering politics.

After we'd been at Kampi Moto for some time, as a result of the Carter Land Commission the Uasin Gishu Maasai were told to move out. I then went down to Ngong and applied for land there. I went back to tell my father, but when I arrived in Nakuru I heard that he was ill. I went immediately to the farm. He was very happy to see me and said he felt better, but after two days when he didn't improve I took him to Nakuru to see a doctor. He died there. My mother, who was living in Mau Narok, died two years later.

I was exceedingly lonely after my father died and I felt it was useless to carry on farming. I hadn't very much experience and didn't think I was capable of carrying on farming on my own. So I sold everything we had and sent most of the money to my brother and sister [by my father's second wife] who were in India and went to Nairobi to look for work. This was in 1935.

## To Somalia and Back

On the second day on which I looked for work I got a job in the Medical Department of the old KAR Hospital [a hospital mainly for Africans]. I was a clerk. I lived at Eastleigh, where the present Kenya Air Force Base is located.

I stayed there until 1941, when I enlisted with the British Military Administration in Somalia. I was appointed as a clerk/typist at the headquarters in Mogadishu. It was during my time in Somalia that I learned Italian. After about nine months, I was made chief clerk, and I acted in that role until 1948, when I resigned to enter business with an Indian friend who used to work at Barclays Bank. We were exporting dik-dik skins, cheetah skins, leopard skins, and python skins—much to my regret today, because my feeling today is that animals should be preserved and not killed. It was a very competitive business with long-established people in it and our business was a failure. I returned to the British Military Administration as a clerk in the Department of Trade. Three months later I was appointed to an officer's grade as Deputy Controller of Imports and Exports. I did work normally done by a European at a salary of £90 a month.

While I was in Somalia I wasn't actually involved in politics but I knew many of the top people in the Somali Youth League and as they didn't know English very well, I used to help them with their petitions to the Government, which was the British Military Administration. One of the people I knew was a clerk under me who subsequently became Prime Minister of Somalia. Later, when I met him as Kenya's Foreign Minister, he used to tell people, 'He was my boss.'

All of us were brought back to Kenya in 1950, but I then went back to Somalia because I had an Italian friend who asked me to join him in a clearing and holding business and I stayed for about two years. But the Italian system was cumbersome and different from the British system, and I got fed up. It was wearing me down and I decided to leave. At the same time I had a premonition that something was going to happen in Kenya, and I thought I should go back home. This was in about May of 1952.

The atmosphere in Kenya was different, people were more conscious of their rights and more conscious of the need for change. They wanted a legislature in their hands, the elimination of the colour bar, more land, and more money spent on education and agriculture.

A previous staff officer whom I knew, who was now a coffee farmer in Kiambu, sought me out and when he found that I was in need of work he spoke to several people. I was offered a job with the CID [the intelligence service] at a very good salary. However, spying on my own people was something I could not do and I refused the job. In the end I accepted a clerical job with a transport business in Nairobi.

When I first came back I stayed with a friend who took me over to a meeting where I asked some questions. When the meeting was over, a young Asian, Pio Pinto, came up to me and asked who I was. Then he told me, 'You must meet all the boys—Bildad Kaggia, Achieng Oneko, and the others in the Kenya African Union.' Gradually I got involved with a group of about twenty KAU members which we called the Kenya Study Circle. We used to meet once or twice a month in Paul Ngai's office or KAU headquarters to discuss Kenya's political and economic problems so that we would be able to brief KAU's leaders.

## Meeting Mzee

The only activity we organized was a conference on the economic problems of East Africa, which we held in Ngei's office on River Road. Mzee Kenyatta came to this meeting and afterward Mzee, who was meeting me for the first time, asked me who I was and whether I was a member of the Kenya African Union. I said that I was not, but that I would become a member, and he told me—I remember these words: 'You must play an active role in the Party.'

After that he used to come very often for car repairs to the Overseas Motor Transport where I was working, and every time he came I would go and say hello to him and he would ask me whether I had become a member of KAU. On the third occasion when I said no he put his hand in his pocket and gave me five bob to pay my subscription but I said, 'No, I'll do that.' So I paid my subscription just three or four months before the Emergency. But I wasn't active at all. I didn't spend any time at all in the party headquarters.

On the day the Emergency was declared, I remember I was sitting at a restaurant down behind River Road, and people were being arrested left and right and put in lorries and taken away; people were being beaten on the streets. And people were being arrested not only in Nairobi but in Mombasa and other towns. When I read that Mzee had been arrested I went straight to KAU headquarters. I found Walter Odede and W W W Awori there, and I asked whether there was anything I could do to help. They told me to come back in the afternoon; they had to elect a new committee. At the meeting, Muinga Chokwe, who was chairman of the Mombasa branch of KAU, was elected as the Acting Secretary. However, as he was wanted by the police, it was suggested that my name be put forward as the Acting Secretary, merely as a cover for Chokwe, which I accepted.

About a week later, I was at the airport to help receive Fenner Brockway and Leslie Hale, British MPs who were visiting Kenya at KAU's invitation, when Chokwe suddenly turned up. Immediately the police saw him they arrested him, and he just had time to give me the keys to the office before he was taken away. As I was on the list as the Acting Secretary General, I was left 'holding the baby', and that's how I entered politics—not by design, but by accident.

CHAPTER TWO

# Emergency and Exile

## When Everything Changed

For Joseph Murumbi, as for many thousands of other Kenyans, the State of Emergency was a major event—perhaps the defining event—of his life. Within a day of its imposition by the British colonial Government on 20 October 1952, Murumbi was embarked on a series of experiences that led to his exile and political career.

The Emergency was a terrified response on the part of Kenya's white settlers to increasing unrest among Kenya's African population. Over the eight years it remained in force, at least 15,000 people—and very likely several times that, almost all of them African—were killed, and hundreds of thousands of African families were displayed.

At the heart of the unrest was land. The growth of the white settler community, aided by British Government loan schemes after World War II, along with a rising African population, made clashes between the settlers and the black previous owners of the land almost inevitable. Moreover, Africans who had served, willingly or otherwise, in World War II, came back with a new awareness of the injustices being done to them and a determination to fight for their rights. By mid-1952, even as Jomo Kenyatta, leader of the Kenya African Union, continued to call for non-violent change, jails were filling with people accused of supporting or perpetrating violence and young militants were slipping away into the forests to take up arms.

## Emergency and Exile

In October, after the murders of a white settler and a black chief, the British Governor at the time, Evelyn Baring, under intense pressure from the settlers' Legislative Council, imposed a State of Emergency. Kenyatta was jailed along with most of the KAU leadership and preparations quickly got underway for his show trial in Kapenguria, a remote town several hours' drive from Nairobi.

When the Emergency was declared, Murumbi had been a member of the party for only three months. Almost immediately he was thrust into the leadership with no preparation. Indeed, by his own admission, 'I didn't know very much about the previous position of KAU and the part people played in it.'

### Needed: A Sense of Humour

One of Murumbi's first responsibilities in his new role was to welcome Fenner Brockway and Leslie Hale, two liberal British MPs who had been invited to Kenya by KAU to observe conditions there. The visitors were greeted by Murumbi and his colleagues along with a crowd of well-wishers. The settlers, however, and the colonial Government, were none too pleased to see them.

Murumbi describes in his reminiscences a meeting at State House shortly before Brockway and Hale met with the Governor in which he and other KAU members were insultingly treated and told in a peremptory manner that they must denounce their leaders. 'The three leaders could not possibly do this,' Brockway later wrote in *Outside the Right*, confirming Murumbi's description of the meeting to him at the time. 'It was wrong, and it would certainly destroy their influence among Africans.' Of their treatment, he comments, 'It is a good thing Africans have a sense of humour. They laughed at the insult.' [20]

Brockway also described in his book an undertaking which, he says, was the 'brainwave' of

Walter Odede, the KAU chairman: Brockway and Hale would write an appeal to the African people, which would be endorsed by Murumbi, Awori, the KAU treasurer, and Odede, and distributed by KAU. In the appeal, Brockway writes, 'We identified with the African demands for land, human wages, education, elected members of the Legislature, elimination of the colour bar. But we also appealed to Africans to disown Mau Mau.' A quote from the appeal contained in *Outside the Right* doesn't mention Mau Mau by name but states that 'Those who in any circumstances advocate a resort to violence, even in circumstances of extreme provocation, are at this moment the real enemies of the African people, not only in Kenya but all over this great continent'.

According to Brockway, as soon as the text had been finished, 'Murumbi went straight to the KAU office to make arrangements for translation, publication, distribution. Three days later this message was being despatched not only to Kikuyuland but to all the tribal reserves of Kenya. I found it ironical that the Kenya African Union, later to be suppressed by the Government, should be the instrument for asking Africans to disavow Mau Mau and violence'[21].

It is hard to square Brockway's description of KAU's disavowal of Mau Mau with Murumbi's descriptions of activities he says he undertook in support of the Mau Mau fighters. It's possible that Murumbi and the others felt they had to appear to the MPs to oppose violence, even if that was not their true position. It's also possible that Murumbi, talking about such events years later, remembered his actions as more militant than they actually were.

If so, this would put him in good company. Over the years, many of those in positions of power changed from their earlier view that the Mau Mau uprising was an ill-advised action of the masses to seeing it as a heroic liberation struggle in which they had played a part.

At any rate, Murumbi had many matters apart from the Brockway appeal on his mind. He describes his early days as a KAU leader as 'spent mostly in trying to organize the defence of Kenyatta and the other members of the party who were arrested with him. And then I went to Kapenguria and I was caught up with that except for weekends, when I used to come to Nairobi, and then I had to go to India'.

The trial itself, in which Kenyatta and the others were charged with orchestrating the Mau Mau activities, dragged on for weeks. Shortly before it ended in April, 1953, according to Murumbi, Kenyatta instructed him to take Kenya's case to the outside world, which he did, starting with a trip to India and Egypt and ending in Britain, where he was to spend nine years.

## A Man with a Mission

One person who met him early on in his travels was Keith Wheelock, who was a 19-year-old student in Cairo when Murumbi arrived there after his time in India. As Wheelock, later a US State Department official, recalls it, the hotel was 'ratty' and the cuisine generally ran to spaghetti and meatballs. But what he remembers most about Murumbi was 'his demeanour, his forthrightness' as well as his command of English. Wheelock recalls Murumbi as 'able to discuss the situation in Kenya dispassionately' and possessing 'a great sense of humour'.

Wheelock says that in his later work in the State Department, he met 'hundreds' of African leaders but Murumbi stands out. 'He was one of the most decent people I've ever met,' he says.[22]

Once in England, Murumbi worked first for the Movement for Colonial Freedom, an activist group supporting decolonization, and later for the Moroccan Embassy.

During this time he was spied on and harassed by British intelligence, as recorded in the British Government's own files, now public, while learning how to petition Parliament, engage in public debates, and become comfortable in front of a news microphone. At the same time, he was meeting dozens of people who would become leaders in the post-colonial world as well as Britain's own political leaders.

All of this would become of great value beginning with the Lancaster House independence talks (1960-1963) and Kenyatta's release in 1961. Murumbi was not himself directly engaged in these talks but what he provided was possibly of more value: a vast knowledge of how things worked, from setting up a press conference to arranging security. He also impressed Kenyatta with his organizational abilities.

It's easy in retrospect to imagine Murumbi's years in exile as useful preparation for his later roles, and to think how heady it must have been to meet leaders like Nehru and Nasser within weeks of setting out on his foreign travels as a virtual nobody. But consider what it must have felt like for him in early 1953 to contemplate leaving Kenya for India with almost no money, no contacts (apart from any he retained from his youth in India), and not even having been on a plane before, and then to learn shortly afterward that KAU had been declared a banned organization, meaning he would be subject to arrest if he ever tried to return home.

Murumbi says very little in his reminiscences about his fears or his doubts in those years, but occasionally a hint of how hard it must have been slips out. Sometimes, he says, when he was living in London and downhearted, he would go to see George Padmore, a Trinidadian Pan-Africanist. 'The first thing his wife used to do was to bring me a glass of cider,' he recalls. 'And then we would have a meal and we would have a talk and I always went away consoled and comforted by George.'

## A 'Dangerous Agitator'

There was also the constant surveillance by British intelligence to contend with, and the claims that he was a communist, or something close to it. The Cold War was at its height, and it's hard to overstate the degree to which both the US and the UK saw the entire world through a Cold War lens.

One entry in a hefty file on Murumbi, kept between 1952 and 1961 by the British Foreign and Colonial Office, states—with heavy use of innuendo and suggestions that the Movement for Colonial Freedom was itself suspect: 'While he does not himself appear to have Communist sympathies, he has inevitably been closely associated with the Communists in the course of his work on behalf of the Movement for Colonial Freedom, and he must therefore, to some extent, be subject to Communist influence. He is certainly a most dangerous agitator.'

As further evidence of Murumbi's dangerousness, another entry in the Murumbi file reports that Murumbi's name was mentioned 'in one of the songs sung by hard core Mau Mau detainees in the Saiyusi Island Detention Camp'.

Officials in Kenya's white colonial Government appeared even more overwrought. Another entry in the file, dated 8 February 1957 and written by Kenyan Secretary for Defence E W M Magor, who had been asked his opinion by London as to whether Murumbi should be allowed to travel as an MCF staff member to Eastern Europe, Tunisia and Japan, reports: 'Apart from Murumbi's activities with the Movement for Colonial Freedom, which is known to have been penetrated by Communists, there is information that he has, at various times, been in touch with Communists in India, Egypt and the USA.'

Recommending that Murumbi not be allowed to go on the trip, Magor continues: 'It is held that this action can be defended without difficulty in Parliament by stating that it is the present policy of the Soviet Union to extend its influence in Africa, and in the first instance this will obviously be done by recruiting Africans, and giving them the necessary training.' [23]

During this same period, in 1954, Murumbi applied for a visa to the United States, after the American Friends Service Committee invited him to speak at a series of workshops around the country. Despite the best efforts of the AFSC, and after a long delay, the visa application was rejected with what appears to have been no reason given. But according to a Central Intelligence Agency document released in 2017 under the Freedom of Information Act, the rejection was based on 'his alleged participation in the Mau Mau movement'. [24]

To read the files of the Movement for Colonial Freedom during the years Murumbi was working there is to hear echoes of every activist struggle around the world: not enough money; constant requests for help, particularly from foreign students; and arrangements for speeches, marches and the printing of endless pamphlets. But the fact is that working with limited resources, from offices in a run-down area near King's Cross, they had impressive success. Stephen Howe notes in his lengthy study of MCF that questions by MPs to the Colonial Office rose by over 70 percent between 1950 and 1957, and by 1957 more than two-thirds of all colonial questions asked by Labour MPs were being asked by MCF sponsors. [25]

One point raised by the MCF files is whether Murumbi's explanation of why he left the organisation is completely accurate. He says in his reminiscences that the reason was a difference of opinion about the appropriate MCF position on the 1956 Suez crisis. But MCF records show an agreement at a February 1957 meeting of the executive committee, at a time of dire financial problems, that Murumbi should be made redundant with three months' pay. [26]

It may be that the decision was altered, or it may be that Murumbi decided to leave of his own accord. In any case the 1957 annual report of MCF says that Murumbi's resignation had been accepted in June 'with great regret'. [27] That the parting was cordial is clear from the fact that Murumbi continued to have a friendly relationship with the organization.

# SAUTI YA KANU

**PEOPLES PRESS LIMITED (IN FORMATION)**
Directors & Editorial Board:— J. S. Gichuru, Oginga Odinga M.L.C., Tom Mboya M.L.C.

FIELD HOUSE
VICTORIA STREET
NAIROBI

P.O. Box 6814
TELEPHONE: 22614

Date 27th March, 1961.

Ref:

My dear Joe,

Forgive me for not having written to you earlier. We were all very busy during the elections. I do not know exactly how well you are informed on Kenya politics. I realise that when one is in Kenya one is liable to become so immersed in its problems as to be oblivious of the bigger problems facing the anti-colonialist forces throughout the world: and by colonialism I imply not merely the political subjugation of a territory but, what may be more important and far-reaching in its consequences, the economic subjugation of a territory, sometimes referred to as neo-colonialism. I realise that when one is in London the problems of Kenya are one of the many problems which one has to face. We here are forced to concentrate on Kenya and its immediate problems because there is little that we can do to affect other issues. You, on the other hand, with all the powerful connections you have built up through your dedication to the cause of striving for the freedom of African states, xxxxxxx are in a position to assist the progressive forces in the Federation and other territories.

Please let me know whether you get the E.A.Standard or whether you would like me to send you cuttings every week by air. I am very anxious that you should be kept reasonably well-informed on the situation in Kenya because it will not be very long before you are called upon to play a much more important part in the affairs of this country. I have sent you two copies of the KANU Manifesto in English. These were printed by me and you will note that I did not forget to include the photos of our real heroes in the long and arduous struggle we have had to wage.

I think Chokwe told you that I and my group are in close touch with our brothers still in restriction - whether at Lodwar, Lokitaung, Marsabit or Hola (now called Galole). J.D. Kali, the last editor of the KAU organ, SAUTI YA MWAFRICA, is now Asst. Editor of Sauti ya Kanu. It will not surprise you to learn that I am working with the old group i.e. Mugo, Chokwe, J.D. and many others who were known to you. I am sure you were delighted to learn of Chokwe's great victory at Mombasa. Although Odede lost badly in the general elections, he secured the highest number of votes for the National seat. F.R.S. de Souza was also elected to one of the two national seats for Asian non-muslims.

In February we started a Kikuyu newspaper called "WIYATHI" which means freedom. The editor is Wilfred Kabue, the old editor of Muramati,

*Letter to Joseph Murumbi from Pio Gama Pinto (1)*

which was banned during the Emergency. Wilfred has recently come out of Galole and was with us in Manda Island.

KANU could have done much better during the elections but it sufferedbadly from indiscipline and personality attacks. Surprisingby, the worst offenders were those who should have known better -the chaps we refer to as the degreewallas. Vicious personality attacks or character assassination, invoking tribalism of the worst type, circulating unsighed scurilous cyclostyled sheets, etc. were all a part of the campaign. Our whole group rallied around Tom, not because we were not aware of some of his shortcomings, but because we all realised the real aim behind the vicious campaign. All of us have our faults and Tom is no exception, but it would have been foolish to ignore his sterling services to the country or to allow opportunists of the first order to take his place. There is much I would like to tell you, Joe, but it must wait until such time as we meet again. The most heartening thing about the whole campaign was that the old Kikuyu political elders -those who were with us in detention at Manda and were the persons who founded the KCA and other organisations- saw through the tactics of these educated tribalists and refused to have anything to do with them. You are no doubt aware of the results.

Although I have been closely involved in Kenya politics, I did not think it was fair to forget our Portugeuse friends!!! Some time before the Santa Maria episode we have been planning the formation of the Mocambique African National Union. There are about 8000 Mocambiquans in Kenya and about 500,000 Mocambiquans in Tanganyika - most of them employed on Sisal estates. As it is impossible for us to organise in Mocambique itself where Portuguese fascism rules supreme, we decided to organise in East Africa firstly. We accordingly held an inaugural meeting at Mombasa and although the Government refused us a public meeting, we launched the Union after a xxxkingxmfx series of meetings with delegates of people of Mocambique origin from a number of places in Kenya, and also from Dar, Tanga and Pemba. Chokwe acted as the convenor.

XXXHHHXX Unfortunately, most of the people who have been forced to migrate from Mocambique are labourers. You are, no doubt, fully aware of Portugeuse policy to deny them any education and to force them to migrate so that they can support the home economy by sending in money and paying their taxes. As such it will be necessary to do most of the organisational work for them in the beginning. We plan to train them and to set up branches throughout the areas where they are found in any numbers. Their lack of education, on theother hand, should not detract from their sense of patriotism and unity of purpose, which is so often found wanting among our so-called miseducated Goans who are never at a loss xxx in producing arguments designed to delay action on every conceivable project.

*Letter to Joseph Murumbi from Pio Gama Pinto (2)*

Among our other activites is to give the maximum publicity to Portugeuse attrocities in Mocambique. Angola is now on the map, but something must also be done to stir up public opinion on the conditions in Mocambique and to assist the Mocambiquans in their struggle against the Fascist dictatorship. Through the E.A.Goan League we have been in touch with Mr. Nyerere and have been assured full support. I understand that a conference is to take place at Casablanca. If there is a possibility, Chokwe and I would very much like to attend the conference. I received a return ticket from the Egyptian Govt. to attend the All African Peoples Conference currently being held at Cairo, but gave my ticket to a KANU Legco. member by the name of Lawrence Sagini, representing Kisii, as the poor chap was very anxious to go and also because I did not think it advisable to leave Kenya at a time when nearly all the leading Kanu politicians were away. A chap by the name of CABRAL wrote to my brother that they had only one ticket available which they felt should be used by a Mocambiquan. My brother explained the difficulties and I feel that if the object is to get something concrete done for the people of Mocambiquean origin they might be induced to change their minds. Please let me know the possibilities. Cabral, incidentally, works for the Goa League in London.

Before I conclude, a little bit of news of our mutual friends. Kaggia and Ngei are fit at Lodwar. I received letters from both. Achieng is still restricted at Kapsabet. He has asked us to visit him and we have applied for permission. Lawrence Karugo, John Mbiyu Koinange, and Babu Kamau are still at Marsabit. They recently sent a petition to the Govt. complaining of conditions there. Jessie Kariuki and Dedan Mugo, also at Marsabit, were fined Shs.80/- each for violating some stupid restriction imposed on them.

Mugo, Kali, Lilian Njeri (your supporter in Kau days), and many other friends send you their very best wishes.

Should you write anything of a confidential nature, please address it to: Mrs. Emma Gama Pinto,
c/o. Jos Hansen & Schoene Ltd.,
P.O.Box 30196,
Pioneer Building, Govt. Road,
<u>Nairobi.</u>

Wish you all success in the work you are doing.

Yours in the struggle,

Pio

P.S. Fitz, Oscar & Rosario send you their best wishes.

*Letter to Joseph Murumbi from Pio Gama Pinto (3)*

*Emergency and Exile*

## Keeping up with Kenya

One interesting question relating to Murumbi's years in London is how he managed to keep up, in those pre-Internet days, with rapidly-changing political developments at home. During this period Kenya went from being a white-run colony to a country on the verge of independence and Kenyatta went from being a prisoner to the leader of a party that didn't even come into existence until 1960.

Part of the answer, at least in the later years, is probably Murumbi's involvement in the Lancaster House talks on independence in which all the leading African politicians from Kenya participated. Once a lonely exile in a strange land, he was now the man who knew his way around the corridors of power. 'Murumbi liked to portray himself as behind-the-scenes, not attracting too much attention,' says historian Macharia Munene. 'Koinange was much more visible in the UK than Murumbi. But Murumbi could get things done.' [28]

Muthoni Likimani, who lived for a time in the mid-50s in London, says Murumbi was always the one who organised meetings between MPs and visiting Kenyan leaders and helped them understand British politics. 'He spoke very good English,' she recalls, as well as adequate Kiswahili. 'He was cool-headed and quite an effective person. He was a man of action, not a man of talking too much.' [29]

Among the Kenyan leaders who came to prominence while Murumbi was away were the first elected African members of the Legislative Council, who took office in 1957. They included Tom Mboya and Oginga Odinga, both of whom were entering electoral politics for the first time. (Daniel arap Moi was one of only two survivors among those who had previously been appointed members.) Mboya's base was the Trade Union movement, which developed partly as an alternative source of political power after the KAU was outlawed. Oginga Odinga, who had met Kenyatta in the early 1950s, was to his lasting credit the first member to call in the Legco for Kenyatta's return to political life.

It was at the First Lancaster House Conference in 1960 that the Colonial Secretary Iain

Macleod said that Britain could no longer withhold independence in Kenya because of the wishes of the white settlers and met with the Kenya Legco members to plot a new course. By this time Prime Minister Harold Macmillan had already made his 'wind of change' speech—prompted no doubt as much by the increasing difficulty and expense to Britain of maintaining its colonies in the face of rising rebellions as by any concern for African aspirations—and the race for political supremacy in Kenya was on. [30]

Within a short time two new Kenyan parties were founded: the Kenya African National Union, which advocated centralized power and urged the release of Kenyatta; and KADU, which was largely driven by fears of dominance by the larger tribes and which quickly became the preferred party of the white settlers.

In the Legco elections of 1961, KANU won a strong victory but refused to form a Government until Kenyatta was released. Eventually this was done, on 21 August, 1961. Kenyatta became President of KANU, leading his party through the further independence talks in 1962 and 1963 and on to independence in December of that year.

*Murumbi with Tom Mboya and others*

IN MURUMBI'S WORDS

# Emergency and Exile

When the British declared the Emergency and started persecuting people, putting them in detention camps, beating them up to get confessions, going out to the villages and shooting people, hunting them, there was a natural reaction against this sort of persecution. The struggle was something which was a spontaneous reaction of the people; it was not directed by KAU as such.

The settlers panicked—it was the first time their authority was threatened. They had always believed that the African was submissive, passive, and would never rise up. Suddenly this thing exploded and of course they couldn't understand what had happened, they couldn't believe it. They formed themselves into groups with rifles and started killing people. They used to go out to villages and say they wanted to employ people, and they put them in a truck and shot them on the way to the police station. We investigated one of these cases and submitted a report to the Governor.

I myself used to stay in different places every night. People knew me and they used to put me up.

We had to supply the people up in the forest with food and ammunition. We could buy ammunition from town, and we could pinch it. We also had our own spy network. Even before the Emergency was declared, our people were in State House and could pinch files: we would get the files, copy what information we wanted and return the files the next day and nobody ever knew anything about it.

When I left Murgian [the transport company owner he was working for] to join the Kenya African Union I had no pay at all from the Kenyan African Union, but I had to live. Whenever I needed money I went to Murgian and he always helped me and he's never made a claim. When I left for India, poor Murgian was harassed by the police; they questioned him about me and what I was doing in Somalia and all kinds of things. And he stood by me, he didn't let me down with the police or anything.

I hate to say it, he's dead now, but Odede [the KAU chair] wasn't a courageous man. For instance, at a certain point we were planning to blow up a railroad bridge connecting Mombasa to the mainland—it didn't come off—but Odede wouldn't have it at all. So in the end we had to do all our planning just Awori and myself, because we felt that Odede might go and report us to the authorities. But this was an out-and-out war, they were killing our people, and we had to do something to retaliate.

There was a man called Lawrence Karugu, a wonderful man, who was the chairman of the KAU branch in Kiburi House. I called up Lawrence and I said, 'Look here, we've got to plan something about destroying the maize crops in Kitale and Eldoret, but we've got to do it very systematically and sensibly. I want you to get a team of people, and we've got to coach them. We've got to wait until the maize is ripe and the stalks are dry, and see which way the wind is blowing, and then set fire at one or two points and the whole farm will be in flames.' And within a week farms were catching fire everywhere in Kitale, done by teams of Lawrence's workers.

James Gichuru, who was a chief, used to collect money for us as he was allowed a certain freedom of movement. Gichuru used to come in my house at night and leave me funds for the party. Gichuru at one time stood a very good chance of assuming the leadership after Mzee, but I think he unfortunately allowed himself to become the victim of drinking.

*Murumbi welcomes Kenyatta and the Kenyan delegation to London before the Lancaster House talks in 1962*

*Emergency and Exile*

## The MPs Arrive

Only a week after the Emergency was declared we had a visit by two British MPs, Fenner Brockway and Leslie Hale, who had been invited by the Kenya African Union. Fenner Brockway was an old stalwart who took a great interest in the liberation of India and after India's independence he switched his interest to Africa. He was a Member of Parliament for Slough, but he was commonly known as the 'Member of Parliament for Africa' because of his interest.

Just before they arrived, the Emergency was declared. Senior Chief Koinange, one of the founding members of the Kenya African Union, had set aside about a thousand pounds to entertain them, but he was arrested. Brockway and Hale sent us a telegram asking whether, in view of the fact that Koinange had been arrested, they should come or not. We said, come. A big crowd of people assembled at the airport to greet them.

At the airport a police officer said that he wanted to speak to them as he had an urgent message from the Governor. The message was that the settlers were very hostile to the visit, and anything could happen. For the MPs' protection, the Governor was going to provide them with an escort. They accepted that.

There was also the question of whether, with Senior Chief Koinange in prison, they should now stay in town. We had actually suggested that, but Brockway said, 'No, I've been invited by Senior Chief Koinange, and whatever happens I must go stay at his house.'

So, off we went to Senior Chief Koinange's house. The Chief had taken a lot of care to see that Brockway and Hale were properly looked after. He had a special cook, the food was excellent, we were comfortably housed. After a few days, because it was more convenient for them to be in town, we moved them there, to the house of J M Desai. J M Desai wasn't there, he was in India, so it was Mrs Desai and her children. Whilst we were staying at the Desais' house, the whole house was ringed by police; police knew everyone who came in, and at times they'd just come into the sitting room and arrest somebody and take him away. So it must have been a horrendous ordeal for Mrs Desai, but she remained as cool as a cucumber, and as dignified as ever.

We had arranged a program for Brockway and Hale to tour the country. The police officers used to trail us everywhere, and of course it had a double purpose: They wanted to know who was seeing Hale and Brockway, and they'd penalize them. It made people frightened to come to see them.

The first day we stopped for a picnic lunch and we invited the police officers to come and have lunch with us. They refused. But later on, other sections of troops became very friendly. Leslie Hale was a very jovial person. He used to crack jokes, and whenever we stopped they all used to gather around him to hear his jokes. In the end they became very fond of Leslie and very amicable. In fact, the night before Leslie left for England, the police officers were sitting down in the lounge with him, smoking long cigars.

Fenner was a more serious man. He tried his best to get some sort of an understanding with the Government and ourselves, to build a sort of bridge between us as it were. He saw several settlers like Michael Blundell and Ewart Grogan, but they had no interest. And obviously there was no hope of trying to get anywhere with them.

Brockway and Hale were able to see first-hand what was happening in Kenya and to collect information on the Emergency and the conditions that prevailed in Kenya at the time. They were then able to report back to their party and the Prime Minister in UK. They also did a lot of speaking. Fenner Brockway wrote a pamphlet called 'Why Mau Mau?' which explained what had actually happened. And they wrote articles in various newspapers in England telling about what they had seen in Kenya. So their visit did have an effect in helping us.

I learned much later that Koinange was in failing health in prison. By then I was in London along with Chief Koinange's son, Mbiyu Koinange. He wanted to see his father and he applied at the Colonial Office for permission and at first they refused him. He was finally given permission, but he was allowed to see his father for only about an hour or so, no more than that. This shows you the cruelty and the lack of humanitarian feelings within the Colonial Office. These are the things that the British people must be made aware of, that the colonial regime was never humanitarian; they made all sorts of claims that they were humanitarian—they had hospitals, they looked after people and this thing and that thing—but incidents like this one show them in a very bad light.

When I came back to Kenya, the first thing I did was to go to Kiambaa and place a wreath of flowers on the old man's grave.

*Emergency and Exile*

## No Shaking Hands with the 'Natives'

Evelyn Baring arrived in Kenya as Governor just as the Emergency was declared and I think the settlers got hold of him straight away and decided that the best thing for Baring to do would be to bring British troops in. The troops arrived and started first with 'Operation Anvil.' Any Kikuyu, Meru or Embu found in Nairobi was arrested. People were arrested by the thousands and taken off to detention camps—not because they had committed any crime but because they were of the Kikuyu, Meru, or Embu tribes.

The British troops were young people and they were shown photographs of Mau Mau, bodies mutilated by the Mau Mau, and told, 'If you don't shoot them when you see them, this is what is going to happen to you.' So these young fellows got frightened, and they shot anything that moved. And this went on, and naturally you can't expect people not to react. Then these various scattered groups of people joined up and joined hands and when the Government had control over the area where people were living, the people went into the forests of Mount Kenya and they carried on the fighting there. And then you got these terrible bombings. They brought British aircraft here and started bombing the forests. People were practically unarmed; they just had homemade guns or maybe a few rifles.

I have a very poor opinion of Baring, because he never showed himself to be a strong character. He represents a type of Englishman who is completely out of touch with the sentiments, the feelings, of people, and is carried away by imperial grandeur. They have to rule, they are destined to rule, and rule they must. But whether they rule with a firm hand or they rule with justice is quite a different matter. I think he was so much under the influence of his officials and the settlers that he didn't know how to handle a situation of this kind. And one must remember that the settlers had a very strong lobby in the UK, and Baring, having that in mind, gave way to their demands on several occasions.

Oliver Lyttleton, the Colonial Secretary, arrived here just shortly after the Emergency was declared and the Kenya African Union prepared a memorandum to give him. We didn't ask for independence, but asked for the Legislature to be half African and the other half non-African; we asked for elimination of the colour bar, more money on education and agriculture, more land, and things of that kind. A week after we submitted the memorandum, we were called to State House, or Government House as it was called in those days.

We were taken in by the back door into the room which is today the Cabinet Room and we sat down. We had worked it out that there were six of us—there was Odede, Awori, and myself, and three members of the committee—and each one was to speak on a certain section of the memorandum and we expected to get an answer from the Colonial Secretary.

When Lyttleton and the Governor walked in, we naturally stood up and said, 'Good morning, sir.' It was normal that Governors would never shake hands with Africans, and Lyttleton didn't shake hands with us either.

The Governor said, 'Now, we've read your memorandum and we're asking you to cooperate with the Government.' And we said, 'But we've come here to find out how we can cooperate with the Government. If you would let us know how we can cooperate, then we're willing to hear.'

The Governor said, 'Well, the first thing you should do is to denounce your leaders.' So we said, 'By asking us to denounce our leaders, you're asking us to cut our own throats. We're asking to be able to talk to the people, hold public meetings, and thereby try and convince the people that violence is not the answer. But we cannot denounce our own leaders.' And besides that, I told the Governor, 'You must understand more than we do that one of the basic rights is a fair trial. As far as we are concerned, they are innocent men; what you're asking us to do is to prejudge them.'

Lyttleton got up and walked out, followed by the Governor. That was the end of the interview. We got no answer to our memorandum. They ignored everything we wrote in the memorandum. They weren't prepared to answer any questions at all. They wanted us to be stooges of the Government, which we were not prepared to do at all.

Well, it hardened us. There were appeals to the British Government, appeals to the Colonial Secretary, and appeals to the Governor, but they had no effect at all. The only alternative was to fight.

## Tea at Kapenguria

When the Government announced the trial of Kenyatta [in late 1952], they informed KAU and said that if we wished to send a representative to Kapenguria we could do so. There were two lawyers: Dudley Thompson, who was a lawyer from Jamaica, and Achhroo Kapila, a local lawyer, and I. [Several more lawyers joined subsequently.] We left Nairobi, spent the night in Kitale at an Indian's house and the following morning we motored on to Kapenguria. We were told that ten miles before reaching Kapenguria there would be a road block and we should identify ourselves there and go through. Just before we arrived at the roadblock, we started to be accompanied by about thirty motorcycles. It appeared that they were all armed with shotguns. We didn't know it at the time but there was also a light airplane following our cars.

At the barrier, I produced my passport, the others produced driver's licenses and things, and they let the two lawyers through. Then they said to me, 'We have no authority to let you in.' I said, 'But that was all arranged in Nairobi.' They said, 'No, we've not been given any authority.' So the lawyers went on and the police told me they would get onto the wireless to Nairobi and find out what had happened. I waited and waited and waited and then a friend of mine from a close-by village invited me to have a cup of tea. As he was preparing tea, the policeman called me and I went back to the police post. And the field officer said, 'Where have you been?' I said, 'I've just been to have a cup of tea.' He said, 'No, you are not to go anywhere, sit down outside here.' He didn't even offer me a chair, I just sat down on the grass. I said, 'Why can't I have a cup of tea?' He said, 'Don't argue, you're in a closed district, we can arrest you.' [Eventually he was allowed to accompany the lawyers each day to Kapenguria.]

The police were after us all the time. On one occasion, I remember, I had just come back to Nairobi from Kapenguria so I had my passport with me. I never took a *Kipande*, that's one thing I want to stress. Since the time I came to Kenya from India, then went to Somalia and came back, I refused to take a *Kipande*. The *Kipande* was an identification sheet which had your thumb impression on it. I was staying at Pumwani at a friend's house, and somehow the police knew I was there. About two o'clock in the morning a police officer entered this room and ripped my blanket off. I got up and there was a torch in my face. He asked me who I was. I said I'm so and so. I asked him, 'Why are you disturbing me?' He said, 'Where's your *Kipande*? Could I have a look at your *Kipande*?' I said, 'You want my passport?' So I gave him my passport. He went outside. They were in wireless communication with Police Headquarters. They had some conversation and he came back to me and gave me my passport and said, 'All right, go to sleep.' They couldn't do anything, they couldn't arrest me for anything. But that's the sort of attitude the police officers had, just like in South Africa. Conditions were the same, you had to carry the *Kipande*.

I saw Mzee almost every day of the trial, but the only thing he said to me, and this is something which may damn the Old Man if I say this, but he said to me, 'Please go and tell

*Daniel arap Moi (third right) and Henry Cheboiwo (third left) visit Jomo Kenyatta (centre) and four others arrested with him*

these people to stop this fighting. This will take us nowhere.' I said, 'How can we do it? It's reached a stage now that if we tried to say anything the people would butcher us.'

My main function during the trial involved the defence lawyers, giving them assistance in finding witnesses. I also used to help Kenyatta and the others. They were getting very poor prison food there and I had to bring them bread and some sausages and bacon and whatever they required. I used to buy the items at Kitale. The defence lawyers were led by Dennis Pritt. Pritt was very left wing, he was probably a communist as a matter of fact, but as a human being he was a decent man who stood up for all the things that we'd all been fighting for.

Every weekend we used to go back to Nairobi because the only telephone we could use in Nairobi was the one at the Indian High Commissioner's, and we knew it was always tapped. We had no other means of communication. But invariably when we urgently wanted somebody to be a witness in our case; when people went to find him he had been arrested and taken away.

We were all except for Pritt living in one long room. Now, I snore very badly, so the poor lawyers couldn't sleep. So I was instructed that I should read until they had all gone to sleep and when I went round and saw that everybody was fast asleep, then I could sleep.

## 'Integrating' Kitale

On one occasion, Pritt, who was staying at the Kitale Hotel, invited us for dinner. It was a hotel which did not admit any Africans or Asians. So we said, 'We'll have a go at it.' Pritt met us at the door, took us in, and asked us to have a drink. He ordered drinks and we had our drinks and then he took us into the dining room.

As we entered the dining room, we could see the faces of the settlers. You could have heard a pin drop. We had our meal; nobody objected. After the meal we sat down to have a few drinks and the manager came to Pritt and called him aside and said, 'Mr Pritt, look here, I don't mind your friends having food in the hotel, but it's against the law to serve Africans with drinks.' It was a silly thing in those days—an African couldn't drink any alcoholic liquor like whisky or brandy or anything of the kind. Pritt said, 'Well, you've already served them, they've had a drink, and there's nothing I can do about it and nothing you can do about it.'

Most of the spectators in the court were local settlers from Kitale. Sitting behind me was a lady called Mrs Mumford; she was reporting for the *Spectator* [a British publication]. She got on speaking terms with us and one day out of the blue she asked us to have a meal with her and her husband at the Kitale Hotel. We told her the difficulties we had had with Pritt. The next day she said, 'We are not having a meal at the Kitale Hotel, we are having a meal on a farm.'

We all went there to the farm and had a very pleasant evening. There was no colour bar there, there was no feeling of resentment to ourselves, and the farm owner was a really genuine person. He welcomed us and we had a meal, we had drinks, and we came back to Kitale about two o'clock in the morning having had a very pleasant evening.

This farmer suggested that we ought to meet the settlers in Kitale, so he arranged for a party for us. All the settlers were introduced and then they shook hands with us, but with a certain aloofness. Gradually as the party warmed up we broke up into small groups and started discussing the political issues of Kenya. The suggestion came out, I don't know from whom now, but instead of having these groups of Europeans, Asians and Africans in Kenya, each one in a watertight compartment, we must get closer to one another. So it was decided that we should form, in every main town, committees composed of Europeans, Asians and Africans, and when there was any issue involving the three races, this committee would get into action and try and resolve it.

On our way back to Nairobi we had a meeting at Nakuru and Diwan Chaman Lal, the Indian lawyer who had joined the team, mentioned this idea, and the next day there was a denial in the paper from Blundell, saying that the Europeans would have nothing to do with this. Some years later, I confronted Blundell. 'Why did you do it?' I said. 'Oh,' he said, 'I don't remember it, I must look up my papers.' I said, 'Blundell, you know very well that you did make this statement and here was an opportunity for us to come together and resolve some of our difficulties and you, who claim to be a liberal, have no idea of being a liberal at all.'

After the trial had been going on for a very long time Chaman Lal talked to Ian Henderson [a colonial police official] and said, 'Look here, Henderson, Kenyatta's not guilty at all and you just want to convict him. Why don't you call off this trial?' I think Henderson was very sympathetic and he said, 'I'll do what I can.'

When we came back on one Monday morning from Nairobi Henderson said, 'I've spoken to the Governor, there's one thing I want to make clear. The Governor doesn't want this to be known by the Attorney General. I will be the medium conducting whatever we discuss to the Governor and I will let you know the Governor's reply.'

This discussion went on for a few weeks until one day Henderson came back on Monday morning, furious with us. He said, 'The talks are called off. You people have not kept your side of the bargain.' The fact that these conversations were taking place had become known to the Attorney General. We knew none of us were in contact with the Attorney General so the leak hadn't occurred from our side. Finally, we found out that the leak had come from the Indian High Commissioner's office. Apa Pant, the High Commissioner, had confided this information to another prominent Indian lawyer who was very friendly with the Attorney General. So the leak occurred there, not from our side at all.

The trial was just a sham. Kenyatta and the others were sentenced and although we appealed and the appeal went to London, we lost all along the line. As a matter of convenience, the Government can manipulate the law to suit themselves. We did put up a very strong case. The defence lawyers were not lacking in any respect. But it was a foregone conclusion, as far as the British Government was concerned, that the man has to be convicted. They had to justify the oppression and the exploitation of people here, they had to find a scapegoat. And that was Kenyatta. At any cost, Kenyatta was to be convicted to justify to the outside world that there was an evil man in Kenya who had caused all this trouble so it was not their fault.

## Leaving for Parts Unknown

Whilst I was at the trial, my visit to India was planned. Kenyatta felt that I should go out of the country and speak to people in India, in Cairo, Britain, North America and West Africa about the situation. The discussions were very secret, because if the Government knew that I was going to India for political reasons they would arrest me before leaving. The India High

Commission knew about it, because they sent messages to Delhi that I was coming.

The Indian High Commission had arranged with Air India that they should reserve a seat for a passenger on a flight to India on such and such a date, without giving the name. I went to the ticket office at about five o'clock when they were closing. There was only one clerk there. I said, 'Here's the money for my ticket.' He said, 'I don't know anything about your ticket.' I said, 'Well, you take the money, go to the manager's house, give it to him, and tell him that this person will collect his ticket tomorrow morning at the airport.'

So he did that. The following morning, H O Davies [A Nigerian lawyer who was part of the Kenyatta defence team] was leaving for Rome. It was quite natural for me to be at the airport to see him off, along with Odede, Awori and a crowd of about twenty or thirty people. The manager of Air India quietly slipped my ticket into my hand as they were all milling around. There were no immigration checks of the sort that you have nowadays. All you did was you sent in your baggage and waited until the announcement came and then you just walked onto the plane.

After H O Davies' plane left, we continued milling around and then the announcement came for the departure of the Air India plane. I walked out. The plane was parked about a hundred yards from the air terminal, and that was the most crucial moment. I was expecting that at any moment someone would tap me on the shoulder and say, 'Hey, where are you going, you're under arrest?' But nothing happened. I got into the plane, my first plane trip, and the plane taxied off.

When I arrived in New Delhi there was a huge reception committee there, people from the Foreign Office and various ministries. I was garlanded and had a press conference. I went to Chaman Lal's house, and that afternoon I met Prime Minister Nehru. He was really a remarkable man, a man who I think was one of the world's greatest leaders. I had a talk with him for over an hour, and he was very sympathetic. He arranged for me to speak to the Congress Parliamentary Group and he also entertained me to dinner at his house. It was the first time I met Indira Gandhi; as his daughter, she used to look after his household affairs.

After a week Diwan Chaman Lal got a telephone call from the Information Officer at the British High Commission saying that he would like to come to see him and could he bring the Reuters man with him. When Chaman Lal told me about this I said, 'Diwan Chaman Lal, they are not coming to see you, they are coming to see me to try to find out from me what is going to happen.'

Chaman Lal is a seasoned politician and when these two gentlemen arrived and started asking me questions, he would butt in and answer them. I didn't say a word. So they were rather disappointed, I think. They started inviting me to parties at the British High Commission. They thought that if I drank I would probably open up and talk to them. So I was very careful; I'd go to the party and have one drink when I arrived and I wouldn't touch another drop.

Then the High Commissioner invited me to see him. I said: this is the best opportunity for me to open up and tell him exactly what I feel. I went and I told him what I felt about Kenya, what I felt about British policy, what we were trying to do, and that we were getting no response from the British in the Kenyan Government, or even the British Government.

When I went later to the Colonial Office when I was in London there were two files nearly two or three inches thick on the table, files about me and my visit to India; there were press cuttings and all kinds of things. They kept a very careful watch on me.

While I was in India it was arranged that I should meet the Indian Parliamentary Group and speak to them. I got very emotional in my speech because it was the first time I had made a public speech. I told them about the brutality of the British forces, the policy, the settlers, and so on. After my speech Nehru spoke with vehemence and disgust about what the British were doing; he made a terribly anti-British speech. Following that he called up the British High Commissioner and lodged a protest about the trial of Kenyatta and the treatment of the Africans in Kenya.

The trip to India helped the cause in the sense that there was a lot of publicity in both Delhi and Bombay, and it made people aware of what was happening. Meetings were arranged, I spoke to various groups, and I broadcast on All India radio.

Odinga was also visiting India at the time I was there, but I didn't know him at all, and not knowing him I was rather cautious. I had never met him in Kenya, so I didn't know very much about him. If he was active in Kenya politics he should have been one of the first people to step forward when we formed the new committee of the Kenya Africa Union and he should have joined us at that time. I don't know at whose instigation he was in India or who sponsored the visit. I met him once and that's all.

## On to Cairo

When I arrived on Air India at Cairo airport, it was about one o'clock in the morning. Before leaving Delhi, I had met a man who later became the first Tunisian Ambassador in London. He was also a refugee staying in Delhi, propagandizing for his country. He was a wanted man; if he'd gone back to Tunisia he'd have been shot. He knew I was going to Cairo and he said, 'I'll tell my people in Cairo that you are coming and to meet you and give you any help.'

When I arrived at Cairo Airport, I looked round for these Tunisians but I didn't see any of them. Then, I was told by the station officer of Air India there that they'd booked me into a hotel. There was a vehicle to take me there. So I went to the hotel, which was on the banks of the Nile, and the first thing I asked was how much it cost for a day. I calculated that I could spend at most three days in Cairo with the money I had and then I'd have to get out. I had a ticket right up to London.

Next morning my Tunisian friends turned up. They saw my room and they said, 'Look here, you're staying in a very small room, you must move from here and take a bigger room.' I said, 'No, I'm quite all right here, don't worry about me.' If I'd had a bigger room, I'd have had to leave Cairo that night.

The Indian Ambassador came to see me and he told me, 'Don't worry about your stay in Cairo.' He had instructions from Delhi to look after me and pay all my bills. So I felt much relieved.

Through my Tunisian friends, arrangements were made for me to see Mohammed Naguib. The revolution had taken place and Gamal Abdel Nasser and Naguib had taken over and Naguib was Head of State. He was a very simple man and a very good man. I also met Anwar Sadat, who at the time was the editor of the *Al Gomhuria*, the Egyptian paper, and I met several other officials. I also met the Algerians and I met the Muslim League people. They were all very sympathetic about Kenyatta. And the Egyptian press went to town with publicity—so much so that the British were embarrassed with the publicity the Egyptian press was giving me. I stayed in Cairo for a month.

Nasser had a very deep understanding and sympathy for the African cause. Later, at many OAU conferences for heads of state, Nasser took a very firm stand on African issues. Whenever we were in Cairo and we wanted to see him he always saw us. He always invited us for lunch or dinner to his residence and talked to us there.

Nasser was a very straightforward man. But many times when I was Foreign Minister I complained to Nasser about the arms given to Somalia which they used to supply to the *shifta* who were fighting against us. Nasser used to say, 'Oh well, these people appealed to us for arms and we gave them arms, but it was on condition they shouldn't use them against anybody else.' I said, 'Well, unfortunately, they are using them against us.' We knew this because we had captured some of the arms and these arms' origin was Cairo. I don't think that Nasser did anything about it.

Maybe it was for their own reasons, but the Egyptians did help us to a certain extent. During the Emergency, many people actually walked from Mombasa; they followed the coast and walked and walked until they reached Somalia. The Somalia Government and the Egyptian Government arranged that they should be flown to Cairo and they got jobs there. So there were quite a number of Kenyans in Cairo.

The Egyptians had a conference on Africa and many representatives came from different parts of Africa. Some of our boys in Cairo attended the conference and they were accepted as Kenya representatives. They appealed to the Egyptian Government and they got an office there, they were given homes, they were given an allowance; all the office expenses were paid by the Egyptian Government. And they also had the use of Egyptian radio and they used to broadcast to Kenya. When I was in Cairo the Egyptian papers were full of news about Kenya.

## *Early Days in London*

When I arrived in London, I spent a very pleasant weekend at the West African hostel, WASU, and also gave the students a talk on Kenya and what was happening during the Emergency. On

Monday morning I reported to the Indian High Commission where one of the secretaries told me that he had instructions from the Indian Government to give me an allowance of eight pounds a week for a year. He also gave me about fifty pounds with which I was to buy some warm clothing as it was September and it would be progressively getting colder.

The Congress of Peoples Against Imperialism, the chairman of which was Fenner Brockway, had arranged a program of meetings for me right throughout the country but as I was late in coming they had to reorganize the program and this took some time. So I spent the first month in London going about to see the museums and art galleries, which I found very interesting. And, with the little money I had, I started buying books.

I also made contact with some of the foreign students who were there in London, and contacted some Quaker friends, who arranged for me to have a meeting with the Colonial Secretary. I was supposed to be the KAU representative in London. When we arrived, we were told that I couldn't see the Colonial Secretary but that a Mr Barton would see me.

When Mr Barton came in he shook hands with the two Quakers and ignored me. He said down and said in a very rough voice: 'Murumbi, I'd like you to understand I've been in Kenya for twenty years.' I looked at him and said, 'That is perfectly obvious.' He asked me what I meant by this. I pointed out what he had done and said, 'That is the attitude of the European in Kenya, who does not shake hands with an African.'

I had prepared a short note of the points I wanted to discuss, which were mainly concerned with the release of Jomo Kenyatta and talks with him and other African leaders about ending the State of Emergency. All my suggestions were of no avail.

After the interview I asked Mr Barton where he had been stationed. He replied that he had been a District Commissioner and mentioned a number of places including Eldama Ravine. I told him I'd been born there and asked if he knew the reason for the nine-foot stone wall around the DC's house. He didn't know, but he remembered the wall. So I told him, 'The reason for that wall was that my grandfather disliked the British and attacked the District Commissioner's house and nearly killed him.'

After a month in London I started a succession of meetings throughout the country. They were mostly with Trade Unions, Labour Party groups, university Labour clubs, and also some Conservative clubs. I spent a whole year going from place to place holding meetings.

I had an invitation to speak to the Kenya Committee but declined after learning that it was a communist group. If I had, I'd have been branded by the Colonial Office as a communist. They were doing everything they possibly could to undermine my work. What I am is a socialist, and not a communist.

Rev. Michael Scott once told me, 'Joseph, there's some rumours floating about that you're a communist; you must have a press conference to deny that you're a communist.' I said, 'Look here, Michael, you're asking me to do something which is stupid. I am not communist. I have never been a communist and I'm not going to go on a platform and say am not a communist. For what reason? That will only provoke discussions by people doubting whether I'm a communist or not.'

I rented a small room in a flat in South Kensington which was owned by a teacher. One day the charwoman, a German, came to me very agitated and said, 'What crime have you committed?' I looked shocked and said, 'I haven't committed any crime.' I think she believed me, because she took me to another room, drew the curtain very slightly, pointed outside, and said, 'You see that car out there? There are two policemen in it who have been watching you for two or three days.'

## 'Termites' in the House of Commons

In 1954 we formed the Movement for Colonial Freedom. The movement was sponsored by nearly a hundred and twenty Labour MPs and many other distinguished individuals. The chairman was Fenner Brockway. Douglas Rogers was the Secretary.

I was appointed Assistant Secretary. This gave me a lot of scope, not only to help my own country, but at the same time to gain a general idea of the [anti-] colonial struggle throughout the world. We put out a lot of pamphlets on various colonial issues and were in touch with area councils and worked with committees which covered the whole of the colonial world. On these committees were MPs who had a particular interest in an area, together with a number of students. We met regularly in the House of Commons, in rooms that were just below the main debating room. I liken our activities to termites who operate underground. These committees met from time to time and briefed the MPs concerned, who in turn raised questions in the House of Commons. This became a very effective weapon against colonial misrule.

I got letters from detainees by a circuitous route, they never came directly to me but through a certain address and they'd be forwarded on. Mbiyu Koinange used to get some information, too, from individual students. There was also a Quaker lady, Eileen Fletcher, who brought back a lot of information on the conditions in the detention camps. And Fenner Brockway handed me a lot of Pio Pinto's reports. How Pio found the time to do all this is remarkable. We know he was dedicated. He believed in the cause, he was more African than many other Africans, and he used his intelligence and training very effectively in providing the information that we needed in London and that we used as the basis for questions in the House of Commons.

We kept very close contact with the press and Fenner Brockway used to have a lot of press conferences. The *Manchester Guardian* always supported the Africans in Kenya and other colonies. The right-wing conservative papers like the *Daily Mail* and the *Telegraph* were not very sympathetic. But I think on the whole we had quite good press coverage.

I met Mbiyu Koinange after I'd been in London two months—he invited me to lunch and he said he must have the truth about Mr Kenyatta. I said Mr Kenyatta was in prison now, he's fought for his country, at least respect him. But Koinange was very critical of him. For some reason or other he preferred to work on his own. There was hardly any coordination between Mbiyu and myself. Occasionally he used to write letters to somebody in the Colonial Office, or Lord so-and-so, but he was never actively involved in the organisation. We'd arrange meeting after meeting for him but he would never turn up. Our own Kenya students were very active.

The information about the Hola massacre [beatings and deaths of Mau Mau detainees in 1959 that the colonial authorities tried to cover up] came out in the press first. And gradually information started trickling through. There were some Europeans who served in the Security Forces in Kenya and who were appalled by what was happening there, and several of them came and told us what the Security Forces were doing in Kenya.

The British Government very skilfully camouflaged their activities in Kenya, but things got through gradually. And part of this, I should say the credit for this, is due to the work the Movement for Colonial Freedom. It exploited not only the Hola incident, but the whole of the colonial actions in Kenya, the British attitudes in Kenya, so people in England became aware that something was radically wrong. There were also other bodies like the Africa Bureau that were working towards these objectives. And within the Conservative Party there were many liberal-minded Conservatives who realized that things were going wrong in the colonies, that morally it was wrong to keep on supporting the settler minority in Kenya.

The public awareness of African people's desire for independence was growing stronger and stronger every day. I don't credit the working man in England with deep insight into these issues, but he is sometimes emotionally moved by these problems and gives them his support. Whereas, on the other hand, you get Conservatives who are influenced by their leaders who have a vested interest—for instance businesses in South Africa, businesses in the colonies—so these affect their judgment. But there were some decent Conservatives who did not openly support us but they gave us their support in area councils and so on. And we had considerable support from the Liberals. Later we had to fight with the Labour Government to get any help. Kenya got its independence during a Conservative Government, and as a matter of fact we got our independence a year earlier than expected.

## The Wider World

Whilst I was in the MCF we made contact with most of the colonial leaders and that made my later task as Foreign Minister much easier because I knew them on a personal level: Milton Obote of Uganda, Julius Nyerere of Tanzania, people like that, and Nkrumah. I also met a lot of leaders at the first All-African People's Conference in Accra in 1958, on the first anniversary of Ghana's independence. At that time, George Padmore was Kwame Nkrumah's adviser in African affairs, and I think it was largely through his inspiration that Kwame agreed to hold this conference.

For the first time we met African leaders whom we'd known only in name, because they were present at the conference. I was most honoured to meet Lumumba and as a matter of fact in my archives I have his card: 'Patrice Lumumba, Secretary General of Le Movement du Congolese'. It was such an enlightening, inspiring conference that it gave the political parties the extra energy to struggle even harder for independence.

There are certain interesting highlights to the conference. For instance, there was a demonstration in support of President Kenyatta who was still in jail at the time. Julius Kiano [later a Minister] was on the platform speaking about Kenyatta's detention, and at a certain moment he was to unfold a placard which said, 'Free Kenyatta Now', except that in his excitement he unfolded the placard upside down.

Kwame wanted to be head of a United States of Africa, but I told him, 'Kwame that is impossible'. What he was trying to achieve was a house starting with the roof, there was no foundation at all. And of course the OAU conference turned the idea down.

But Kwame was very farsighted. Although he was reckless with money, he spent money on some schemes which were designed to build the infrastructure of Ghana's economy, and in building the infrastructure you don't get immediate results. For example Tema Harbour, which was built by Kwame, is now doing a tremendous volume of business, because Accra itself is not suited to be a deep-water harbour.

I remember a time when MCF was in debt to the extent of about £900, and Douglas and I decided that we would both cut our salaries by half. Douglas was drawing ten pounds a week, and I was drawing eight pounds a week. We maintained this cut for about nine months. I was living at Muswell Hill, which must be about five or six miles to King's Cross, where our office was situated. So I had to study the road maps and find out the shortest route between my home and the office. Since I could not afford to go by bus, I had to walk there every morning and walk back in the evenings. It did a lot of good for my figure, but not for my shoes.

Canon John Collins is one of the most remarkable people I've ever come across in England. I used to go to see him regularly. He and his wife are both marvellous people who've taken up many causes, including of Africans and people in difficulties.

I had the opportunity of seeing Paul Robeson because John Collins had the courage to invite him to sing in St Paul's Cathedral. One must remember that after the McCarthy era Paul Robeson was not allowed even to sing at any public halls in America. Collins gave me a ticket but something happened and I couldn't go. So when I was in New York years later, Burudi Nabwera, the Ambassador, and I drove to Paul's house. When I saw him, he was as I imagined him to be: big, a very tall man, very well built—but one could see the trace of sadness in his face. He was a broken man.

I still play his records from time to time. There's a particular song which he sings—'Nobody knows the trouble I've seen'—which typifies what he felt in his heart about the American Government's treatment of him. But I think Paul Robeson will go down in the annals of history as a great man, a great singer, a great actor.

*Emergency and Exile*

## An Insular People

On my first Christmas Eve in London I went to see Canon Collins to wish him a happy Christmas. Collins came in, followed by his seven-year-old son, and greeted me as usual, but his son, who had never met me, hesitated at the door. Very quietly, he came up to me, looked at me for a while, and then ran to his mother. 'Mummy,' he said, 'that man hasn't washed his face.' There was a deadly silence in the room; Canon Collins was looking at his wife, and his wife at him. And I burst out laughing.

I said to the little boy, 'Yes, I haven't washed my face, could you take me to the bathroom, and I'll wash my hands, too.' So he took me in and opened the taps. He scrubbed my hands, I washed them, he scrubbed them again, I washed them. He was rather puzzled. When we returned to the sitting room he went to his mother and said, 'Mummy, I washed his hands, but the colour wouldn't come off.'

I used to use this incident very often in my speeches, and I used to equate it with another incident which happened when I was going home from my office at King's Cross. I took the tube at King's Cross Station and after a while a man came in, sat opposite me, looked at me with a look of disgust, and got up and walked way. I then watched him some seats away start an argument with somebody there and come back again to sit opposite me. I took out a cigarette and saw that he was looking at it, so I extended the pack and said, 'Have a cigarette.'

There was the most remarkable transformation in the man. He got up and came to sit next to me and looked at me and said, 'You remember I came to sit opposite you? I was disgusted to see an African, and I got up and went to a fellow-countryman and asked him for a cigarette and he insulted me. And there you are, unknown to me at all, and a stranger in this country, and you offered me a cigarette.' I never met the man again, but this incident, too, shows the insularity of the English people.

Several years later, I visited Paris when I was Foreign Minister of the Kenya Government, as an official guest of the French Government, and I met President de Gaulle. We discussed African politics, Kenyan politics, and then de Gaulle introduced a subject which had nothing to do with Africa: Britain's entry into the Common Market. He told me that he opposed it mainly because the British had always been an insular people; they never felt themselves a part of Europe.

But the British people also have admirable qualities, one of which is that Britain has been a refuge for peoples from Europe, Africa and Asia, people displaced from their countries. Many have remained there for the rest of their lives. Others, like myself, who were agitators, found it a useful refuge where one could condemn the Colonial Government and still be secure, whereas if one said the same things in one's own country one ran the risk of arrest.

I left the Movement for Colonial Freedom because of a disagreement during the Suez Crisis. When Nasser nationalised the canal, the Movement for Colonial Freedom supported the nationalisation of the canal, but then the issue became rather hot and Russia threatened to atom bomb or send rockets to Britain, and the whole campaign moved from support for the nationalisation by Nasser to insisting on no war against Britain. I told them that the role of the Movement for Colonial Freedom was not to be concerned with war against Britain, it was to be concerned with the future of the colonies and the liberation of the colonies. And for that reason, I resigned.

But I continued in contact with MCF and they arranged for meetings for some of our delegations when they came.

When I resigned, I was out of a job for about two weeks, and then I got a job at the Moroccan Embassy through a friend of mine, the Tunisian Ambassador. I was very happy there because the Moroccans treated me like a Moroccan in spite of the fact that they were warned by the Foreign Office that I was a dangerous character and that they shouldn't employ me. I worked as an Assistant Press Officer for the Moroccans practically until the time I came back to Kenya, even during the time that we had our delegations in London for the two constitutional conferences. I was given time off to work for the delegations. I was told by the Moroccans to use all the facilities in their offices, if I wanted, to help our delegation.

# The Wind of Change

When Iain Macleod made the famous declaration [in 1960] that Kenya is an African country and there must be majority rule, the reaction of the settlers was to go to Macleod immediately and ask what the hell he meant by this. Macleod said, 'I mean what I say.' We ourselves were confused because we thought there'd be some compromise formula—that we would get a majority in the Legislature, leading up to independence eventually, but when, we never knew. So we also approached Macleod. Macleod's reaction was, 'Do you people want independence or not? If you don't want independence, I'll withdraw what I said.' We said, 'No, no.' Those few words of his changed the whole history of Kenya.

One must also give credit to the British Prime Minister Harold Macmillan. I don't think anybody has said this, in as many words as I am saying it now, but I think that we are fortunate that there was a change of heart in the British Government. What I mean by the British Government is Macmillan himself. Macmillan made an African tour—he went to West Africa, to Ghana and Nigeria, which were independent at the time—and the people there told Macmillan that Ghana and Nigeria would be in the forefront of the struggle for the liberation of Africa. They wanted those British colonies to be free.

From Nigeria, Macmillan went to Rhodesia, and he had an unfavourable reception there. He went to South Africa after that, where he made the famous 'Wind of Change' speech. I think Macmillan's mind was made up on that trip, and particularly when he went to South Africa, that things would have to change and the British Government would have to concede independence to the colonies in Africa.

I think Macmillan was wise enough to realize that the African people were in the mood for independence, and they would not accept any half measures. If the British wanted to keep them down and deny them independence, they would have to police a very large area in Africa, which they couldn't afford to do. I think Macmillan came to the conclusion that it was better to concede independence to these countries under conditions of good will, maintain the friendship of the African territories thereby, and also maintain what was more important to

Britain: the economic relations with the former British colonies. When Macmillan made up his mind, I think he probably must have persuaded his cabinet that this was the best line. Then he appointed Iain Macleod as the Colonial Secretary to carry out this task.

Macleod was a very shrewd politician and a decent man. I was very, very impressed with Macleod. I met him once or twice, and I met him some years later at Brighton at the Conservative Party Conference. He recognized me and he knew my name; Macleod had a fantastic memory. I'm very sorry he died prematurely, because he would have been, I think, a very able leader of the Conservative Party. He was a man who was liberal in his outlook, he wasn't a diehard conservative like some of the others were. Macleod was appointed as Colonial Secretary to speed up this process of decolonization.

## Serving Kenyatta

When Mzee came to London [for the second Lancaster House talks] I immediately offered my services to Mzee and the delegation. I managed all the delegation's appointments, did all the typing work for them, arranged meetings for them and so on with the press, with other bodies in England, and did sort of public relations work for the delegation. I knew London, I knew the press, and the people whom they should meet—Members of Parliament, both Conservative, Liberal, and Labour—so I was in a position of being able to give them all the assistance possible.

One day, Mzee had his drawer full of letters which hadn't been answered. He asked me to take them all out and see what answers I could give. I took all the papers out and I found two bundles of notes, one of them £5 notes. I didn't know what the amount was but I said, 'Mzee this money was left in the drawer.' 'Oh, yes,' he said, 'I've been looking for this money, I didn't know where it was!'

We also had to provide security for Mzee and this was done by the students in London, because the British Government did not provide any security. There was a policeman on duty, but he was not officially delegated to protect Mzee. Mzee was living in the Cumberland Hotel.

*Emergency and Exile*

The students were lined up along the corridors on both sides so that nobody could come and force an entry into Mzee's room, because there were press men and all kinds of people wanting to see him. I had to be very careful that nobody would harm the Old Man. So that worked quite successfully. Whenever he was leaving the hotel we had him flanked on both sides and also on the front and the back with the students protecting him until he got out and got into the car. He was going to a meeting in the Colonial Office when somebody threw an egg at him. It fell on Mzee's lapel. He was very dignified, he didn't say a word, he just looked at the man who threw the egg, then brushed it off and got inside the Colonial Office and did not refer to it at all.

We had these crazy people called the League of Empire who wanted to create a disturbance. We were having a press conference in the basement of a London hotel, behind Victoria Station, and all the people were seated. Just before Mzee came down the stairs, a policeman came to me and said, 'That lady sitting in the front row is from the League of Empire Loyalists, so watch out.'

I couldn't get her out because Mzee was coming down the stairs and he came in and put his stick on the table and sat down. I stood between that lady and the table and Mzee. Suddenly this lady got up and tried to make a swipe at Mzee with her handbag and I pushed her. She fell back in her seat and didn't strike Mzee. The police got hold of her and took her out.

Then the press conference started. Suddenly, a man toward the end of the room flung a

*Joseph Murumbi with Tom Mboya and others during preparations for the Lancaster House talks in 1963*

newspaper, with what turned out to be offal, at Mzee, and it hit the edge of the table and fell down. We subsequently learned that this man was not from London, he was specially brought from Newcastle-on-Tyne to do the job, and he was an ex-wing commander in the air force. It shows you that even such responsible people had distorted minds. Well, one of our students, Ngumo Njuri, tackled this man and knocked him down and he was taken out by the police.

Patrick Renison [Governor of Kenya 1959-62] was a peculiar character. I met him only once in a hotel in London during the Constitutional talks when he had come there to speak to some of our delegates. He had made that very silly statement that Kenyatta was 'the leader of darkness and death'. I wonder what his reactions were when Iain Macleod said Kenya is an African country and there must be majority rule. In London, Renison was chasing us in the hotels to get us to agree to certain things, while in Nairobi we had to creep and crawl about on our knees to get to the Governor.

The Moroccans gave us money over various periods including during the Constitutional Conference. They came to the Convent Hotel where the Old Man was staying, and they brought a parcel and said, 'Mzee this is from the King, a present for you.' We didn't know what was in it. The Ambassador didn't say very much, he presented it and just said his salaams and he went away. We thought of some silver thing or some little present. When we opened the parcel we saw these new £5 notes. We counted it: £24,000 [equivalent to nearly £500,000 today].

## *Money and Friends*

Odinga is very generous with money and he has helped a lot of people in need. I remember in London he came to us after Mzee was released and said, 'Look here, Mzee, I've got £10,000, you must have some of this money because you've got no money.' He gave the Old Man about £2,000 or £3,000. Nobody sneered at him because it was communist money, we were poor then and we had no money and we welcomed that money and it was paid to us in pound notes, not in dollars. Odinga was very straightforward about it, he never hid the fact of where he got the money. But as far as I know Odinga is not a communist.

He has one virtue, it never fails, that if you've helped Odinga, if you ever did him a good turn, he will never forget it and he will forever be grateful to you and always be your friend.

The division between Odinga and Tom Mboya goes back a long way to the time when Kenyatta was in prison. These two were vying for not only the leadership of the Luo, but also for the leadership of the country. Tom Mboya had support, including financial support, from the Americans, the West Germans and the British Labour movement. He was using this money to safeguard the strength of his own position. I've heard Mboya tell people, 'Well, I owe you nothing, I paid you for what you did for me and that's the end of it.'

Mboya wasn't at all a friend like Pinto, but nevertheless one has to acknowledge that he has played his part in Kenya's history, and very efficiently, and at a difficult time. During the Emergency, when he could have been locked up, he played his cards very well and he was able to keep the political side going, using the Trade Unions in a very efficient manner. One has to pay respect to him for that. And he played a very efficient part in the constitutional talks. I worked very closely with Mboya during the London conferences, and he was the only one who actually worked. Really, he worked. I used to wake up Mboya at seven o'clock in the morning and we went till nearly midnight. We'd go to the conference and in the evening he had his engagements—meetings, press conferences and so on. He did all the writing of all the documents. While other people were having a good time, Mboya was working. And one must accept that, whether you like him or not, he has played his part.

## Looking to the Future

On the night before Mzee left for Nairobi, he asked me to have dinner with him. He had cleared it with the Governor that Koinange and I could return. He told me, 'Joe, now you've got permission to come back to Kenya, what are you going to do when you go back?' And I said, 'Mzee you know I've been away for nine years, and I've got to go back to see my people and friends and then look for a job.' So, he said, 'Now supposing I make a proposition to you to work for me.' I said, Mzee, I'll work anywhere.'

So he said, 'Now you come back to Kenya for two weeks and after the two weeks you'll come back to London [because there was another constitutional conference]. I want you to be present in London. And then you can come back for good.' I agreed. I went home and I spent two weeks seeing all my old friends, and I used to spend practically every second day with Mzee at Gatundu, because he wanted me to be there every day. I said, 'Mzee, I can't be here every day, I've got friends to see.' So, I used to spend every second day with him.

If Mzee likes you, he wants you to be near him all the time. I remember when I was a Minister, I would come home in the afternoon for lunch and I would get a call from him, 'Joe' he would say, 'I've got something to discuss with you. What are you doing?' I would say, 'I'm just sitting down for lunch.' 'Leave your lunch, come and have lunch with me, I've got something to discuss with you.' So, I'd go up to State House, have lunch with him, and he'd tell me, 'Now Joe, sit down here, order any drinks you want, coffee, tea, whiskey, anything you like. I'll see you in a few minutes, I've got something to do.' So, I'd sit down there waiting for him and he'd suddenly come out of the office. 'Oh, Joe, I forgot about you. Wait a minute, I'll see you in a few minutes.' This would go on until about half past four. And then he'd get in his car and he'd go away. He'd say, 'Come tomorrow, I'll see you tomorrow, I've got to discuss something important with you.'

He doesn't want to discuss anything with you, but he wants you to be around. He cannot be lonely. He was kept under solitary confinement when he was detained and the effect of that is that he cannot bear to be alone, he must have somebody around him.

I went back to London after those two weeks. Then, when the Constitutional talks were over, I packed up my books and everything and I came back. Mzee arranged a tremendous welcome for me. There were dancers and bands. I was met at the airport by a very large crowd of people. There was a reception and all that, and then I was taken from there to Parliament Buildings and had lunch with Mzee. After that I had a press conference.

Mzee asked me to meet him the next day at the Parliament Buildings at eight o'clock. I met him and he took me up to his office, which was at Solar House, behind International House. He took me into his office and said, 'Joe, this is my desk. I want you to sit at my desk, deal with all my correspondence. Many people want to see me. If you can solve their problems, you solve them; if you think they should see me, you bring them to me. I leave that entirely to you.'

In the office was Achieng Oneko. I told Oneko, 'Look here, Oneko, you are senior to me, and

I shouldn't sit at Mzee's desk, you should sit there.' I had high regard for Oneko, because he was a great friend of mine, and besides he was the Secretary of KAU and I had taken over from him when he was arrested. So I felt myself junior to him, and I didn't feel it right for me to take Mzee's chair. I think this was something which made Oneko and me very close to each other, because Oneko said, 'No Joe, you sit down there at Mzee's desk, I'll work with you.' We were always very great friends after that.

## Sheila

I met Sheila at a dance at Mbiyu Koinange's house, in London. I had heard that she was a librarian and I wanted to get my library catalogued. Of course, it wasn't very big at that time, I had only about 600 books, and Sheila volunteered to do it. It may be a question of the spider saying to the fly, 'Come to my parlour', but anyway she catalogued my library and we developed a very keen friendship from then onwards.

When I was about to leave London, I told Sheila, 'Look here, we've been great friends now and I feel that I have to go to Kenya, but I don't feel that I can go away and leave you behind. Why don't you come to Kenya with me?' So she got herself a job as a librarian in the Medical Research Laboratory and she came ahead of me by about a week. Mzee Kenyatta had met her in London and he arranged for her to be met at the airport by Margaret Kenyatta, and then driven straight to the Parliament building where he entertained Sheila to lunch. He has always had a lot of respect for Sheila and liked her very much and so did Mama Ngina.

Sheila and I were married according to Maasai custom. The ceremony took part at Lolgorian. Kenya is now her home and she has no intentions of going to England. When she went to London she wrote to me and said she was homesick on the plane going out. One of the advantages of Sheila is that she is very pleasant and very kind to people. I seem to be harsh in some ways but she always has a nice way of dealing with people, a very pleasant way, and people have come to admire her and like her, people of all races. She shares all my hobbies: she likes gardening, she collects stamps, we both like classical music, and of course we both love dogs.

When Sheila was young she had a cat at home, and when I met her she didn't like dogs. But we started having dogs in Kenya and she is now very fond of them. Her favourite is 'Dimple' who would defend Sheila if anybody attacked her because when Dimple was young his mother was knocked over by a car and Sheila brought him up, mothered him. Dimple is forever faithful to her and he sleeps at the side of her bed. We have about seven dogs—three poodles and one pure-bred Labrador and three are mixed and she loves them all.

When Sheila's boss was going away and selling his house on Welbeck Road—a Spanish type of house—Sheila saw it and she was very anxious to buy it, and she told me about it, and took

*Sheila Murumbi, Joseph Murumbi's wife*

me over to see it. I said, 'Well, Sheila, I have no money. I'm drawing fifty pounds a month looking after Mzee's office and the Pan African Press'. Sheila was very anxious about the house, and she was weeping; she said, 'Oh you must buy the house'. I said, 'I can't. The only thing I could suggest is we can sell part of the library and buy the house.' She said, 'No we can't do that.'

So I went to the President and said, 'Mzee, I want you to come and see a house.' So, I took him over and he saw it. This doctor who owned the house had grown so many trees around the house you could hardly see the house from the road. And the Old Man was very fond of trees and said, 'Joe, you must buy the house, look at all the trees.' So, I said to him, 'Mzee, I like the house, but how am I going to pay for the house? You know what I am drawing. I'm drawing fifty pounds. I can't afford it.' I said, 'Can you help me?'

He gave me a thousand pounds, as a gift. And then I approached Odinga; he gave me five hundred pounds. The house cost four thousand pounds, and I was able to put down one thousand five hundred pounds with the insurance company here, and we got the balance of two thousand five hundred pounds, and we bought the house. I paid off the house just after I resigned as Vice-President.

CHAPTER THREE

# The 'Reluctant Politician'

## A Loyal Aide

The Joseph Murumbi who returned to Kenya from England in 1962 was a considerably different person from the one who had left Kenya for India nine years before. At the time of his departure, he was an impoverished representative of a little-known freedom movement, a man who'd never before addressed an audience or been on a plane. But by the time of his return he was a polished speaker, an urbane Londoner who collected art and books, and an acquaintance of world leaders from Nehru to Nkrumah, many of whom he counted as friends.

Murumbi had also gone from being a political neophyte to a sophisticated player, someone who understood not only the politics of Kenya but, thanks to his travels and contacts, the politics of Africa and the world at large. This made him valuable to Kenyatta and his fledgling government in a variety of ways, but perhaps most of all as someone who could get things done.

But what he hadn't acquired, it would seem, is a taste for the rough and tumble of political life. Cyprian Fernandes, a Kenyan of Goan descent who worked as a journalist in Nairobi before leaving the country in 1974, describes Murumbi in his memoir *Yesterday in Paradise* as 'something of an introvert...He found it difficult to talk about himself and even more difficult to talk about the various strands of politics prevailing in the country at the time. I even got the feeling sometimes that he was a reluctant politician.'[31]

## The 'Reluctant Politician'

Fernandes' remarks are echoed by veteran journalist Joe Kadhi, who never dealt with Murumbi in person but edited many political stories involving him. 'In a way he was apolitical,' says Kadhi. 'But he was able to be elected to Parliament because people were very loyal to political parties and he was sponsored by KANU.' He adds that Murumbi was 'highly respected by journalists' and regarded as far brighter than most of his peers.[32]

Duncan Ndegwa, later Kenya's first African head of the Central Bank, was somewhat less impressed. In his autobiography, he calls Murumbi 'a hard worker' but says that 'He was certainly not Mboya's match in fashioning and implementing policy'.[33] Perhaps more telling in terms of Murumbi's political talents, British Colonial Governor Malcolm MacDonald, in a pre-independence summary of the Kenyan political scene, did not include Murumbi in a short list of people he thought most likely to be successors to Kenyatta.[34]

*Tom Mboya, Joseph Murumbi, unknown, Timothy Chokwe, Jomo Kenyatta.*

Such comments suggest that Kenyatta's keenness to recruit Murumbi to assist him may well have been in part because of Murumbi's very lack of political ambition: Kenyatta never had to worry that Murumbi was operating in his own interest rather than that of Kenyatta or of the country at large. Kenyatta was undoubtedly also impressed by Murumbi's considerable administrative talents, seeing him perhaps as the consummate, competent Goan of the sort who were ubiquitous in Kenya's British colonial offices.

Murumbi's attention to detail is everywhere apparent in the papers he left to the Kenya National Archives: a draft of a speech, impressive in its grasp of factual details, with corrections hand-written in Murumbi's tiny, neat, script; a diary with three Kiswahili words, along with their English meanings, carefully written inside the front cover; a notebook dating from 1962 in

*Joseph Murumbi and President Jomo Kenyatta with an Ethiopian delegation*

which the specifics of an upcoming visit to London by Tom Mboya are precisely recorded.

While Murumbi makes a point of describing how much Kenyatta trusted him to carry out foreign affairs and even deputised him to act as Prime Minister on at least two occasions, Murumbi appears not to have been a member of Kenyatta's inner circle. Rather, he was the valued aide—not one of the few who made the big decisions but rather someone who could be relied on to be sure those decisions were implemented.

Murumbi's attitude toward Kenyatta was one of deference and respect; the Kenya National Archives contain many examples of correspondence between the two in which Murumbi always addresses the President as 'Dear Mzee'. (One notable exception was an exasperated letter Murumbi wrote in early 1963 after being instructed by Kenyatta to reorganize the KANU headquarters but not given the funds to do the job. 'I am really disappointed with you personally', he told Kenyatta, who quickly moved to rectify the situation.)[35]

*Murumbi (behind Queen Elizabeth and Prime Minister Harold Wilson) representing Kenya at the Commonwealth Conference, 1966*

## *The Years of Decision*

The period of Murumbi's active political life in Kenya—1962 through 1966—was the most pivotal in Kenya's history, a time when key decisions were being made about what direction the country would take politically and economically. The differences of opinion about these issues between the Odinga wing of the party and the Kenyatta wing are hinted at in the manifesto overseen by Murumbi and issued by KANU before the 1963 pre-independence elections. As one example, the manifesto states that Kenya will have a firm policy of non-alignment and a 'socialist society'—but it also states that 'The Marxist theory of class warfare has no relevance to Kenya's situation. Attitudes which were appropriate when we were fighting for independence have to be revised'. [36]

Meanwhile, dramatic changes in governance structures and personal and political loyalties were also occurring. Over a few years the country moved from being run by a colonial government through a brief era of decentralization after independence and then on to a highly-centralized, one-party system in which virtually all power resided in the Presidency. Oginga Odinga went from being Kenyatta's champion to a bitter enemy; Pio Gama Pinto was murdered; and the tribalism and corruption that would fifty years later lead to a brief but near-catastrophic period of post-election violence in 2007-2008 began to take hold.

Professor Muriuki, who was a student at Makerere University in Uganda at the time of independence, recalls the sense of euphoria on 12 December 1963. 'There was a lot of hope, a lot of expectation. It seemed heaven on earth literally could come,' he says, recalling the Nairobi celebrations. 'We were probably drunk with the feeling that come December 13, everything would change.'

But the euphoria was short-lived, starting with an army mutiny the following month. 'That is where, in my view, things began to unravel,' Muriuki says. 'Kenya was forced by circumstances to seek assistance from Britain but that assistance came with strings attached, one of which was that Kenya would be pro-Western as opposed to supporting the socialist countries.' ³⁷

While certainly no lover of the West, Kenyatta was culturally inclined toward capitalism and the philosophy of individual responsibility behind it. 'Kikuyus believe that if you can't look after yourself, you can't look after the country,' says Muriuki. 'This predates colonialism; it's part of Kikuyu culture.' ³⁸ Duncan Ndegwa in his memoir describes Kenyatta as not seeing

*Njoroge Mungai, Papal Nuncio, Robert Matano, Jomo Kenyatta, Joseph Murumbi*

himself 'as having led a peasant revolution in the socialist sense...The struggle as he saw it was not to liberate the peasants as such but Kenya itself'. [39]

Odinga and many of Kenya's younger leaders, in contrast, were much more inclined to radical ideas about the rights of workers and the distribution of resources, and they saw the Soviet Union as a champion of the developing world. This eventually put Kenyatta at odds with Odinga, who was highly critical of the Kenyatta government's generous buy-backs of land from departing settlers, vocal about the need to help the former Mau Mau fighters, and the recipient of generous assistance from the Soviet bloc.

Murumbi was something of a mix: he had no use for communism as a system of government, but he was deeply concerned about the needs of poor people and always highly sceptical of Western motivations. According to Muriuki, 'Murumbi felt very uncomfortable because he did not support the policies that the Kenya government was taking, particularly in the economic field. He was much more comfortable with the positions taken by Odinga and Kaggia rather than the positions taken by Kenyatta and Charles Njonjo and the others.' [40]

Murumbi was, however, a pragmatist, perhaps best described as a European-style social democrat. 'Welfarism was his cup of tea; do something for the [Mau Mau] fighters', says fellow historian Munene. 'He would have been a supporter of corporate social responsibility'. [41]

*President Kenyatta with Vice President Murumbi and visitor*

## The Cold War in Kenya

Separate from the debate over Kenya's future and its political philosophy, but very much connected to it, was the Cold War. Africa was a highly active sector of that war, which pitted the UK and the US against the Soviet Union and China.

'Once the Cold War hit us was when ethnic balkanization began,' according to Muriuki. 'With Odinga largely supported by Russia, with Kenyatta largely supported by what I call the Mt Kenya mafia, that now brought into focus the problem of ethnicity. We now began to stereotype one another. Luos became the enemies of the state, the enemies of the Kenyatta government.' [42]

Seen through a Cold War lens, when individuals and countries were regarded as 'for us' or 'against us', Western governments clearly saw Murumbi as in the 'against' camp. This was illustrated in the case of the Congo, where civil war had been ongoing since the murder of left-leaning Prime Minister Patrice Lumumba in 1960. During Murumbi's time as Foreign Minister, in 1964, he participated in a failed mediation effort that increased US suspicions that he was not only anti-Western but also sympathetic to what they perceived as pro-communist forces.

In his 1967 memoir *The Reds and the Blacks*, William Attwood, the US Ambassador to Kenya for two years in the immediate post-independence period, criticizes Murumbi for what he perceives as his quickness to denounce Western actions. Describing Murumbi's remarks as Foreign Minister at the UN during the Congo crisis, in which the US and other Western countries backed one faction and the Soviet Union and China backed the other, he writes that Murumbi 'not to be outdone by anybody, declared that "Belgian and American aggressors were wholly and directly responsible for all the excesses that were committed in the Congo"'.' [43] He also claims that Murumbi 'sometimes seemed to be playing Odinga's game'. [44]

Attwood's remarks can be dismissed as a reflection of his intense anti-communism, but he was not alone in his perceptions. Malcolm MacDonald, who became British Governor-General and then High Commissioner after independence, and with whom Murumbi was on a first-name basis, also saw Murumbi as too pro-Soviet for Britain's taste. In a communication of 30 June 1965, MacDonald attributed his failure to arrange a meeting for a visiting British official with Murumbi's Permanent Secretary in the Ministry of External Affairs to 'the reluctance of the Permanent Secretary to be involved in his master's absence in discussion on the subject of Congo, on which Murumbi holds very strongly prejudiced views'. [45]

At times, if Attwood is to be believed, such criticisms of Murumbi fell on sympathetic and highly-placed Kenyan ears. After Murumbi, in a UN General Assembly speech in October of 1965, described US actions in Vietnam as 'the greatest menace to international peace and security', Attwood asked for clarification of Kenya's position. Kenyatta told him, Attwood claims, that 'Joe sometimes exceeded his instructions'. Subsequently, according to Attwood, Murumbi was instructed (by whom he doesn't say) to call on US Secretary of State Dean Rusk and 'clarify' Kenyan policy. [46]

For all of the US criticisms of Murumbi, however, the American CIA—which years earlier had weighed in against granting him a visa—appeared by the mid-1960s to hold him in high regard. An entry for him in the CIA biographic register dated September 2, 1966 (by which time Attwood had left Kenya) describes him as 'outgoing' and a good speaker, as well as 'urbane, intelligent and articulate'. [47]

The differences of opinion between Murumbi and Kenyatta were most pronounced on Rhodesia, a case in which Western fears of communism became intertwined with white colonials' fears of black rule. Murumbi repeatedly tried to get Kenyatta to take a more aggressive stance against the white settlers in Rhodesia after they unilaterally declared independence in 1965, and used his position as Foreign Minister to push a tough line calling on Britain to take over direct administration of the colony, using force if necessary. In a statement he delivered in 1966 at the end of the last conference at which he led Kenya's delegation (and perhaps emboldened by that fact), he told the British Government: 'It is clear to us that this is a matter of economics. You wish to hold on to Rhodesia, avoid the application of mandatory sanctions, and thus save your own economy at the expense of four million Africans.' [48]

But Murumbi's efforts were unavailing. 'Murumbi continued to indulge in anti-British rhetoric throughout the [Rhodesia] crisis and most notably very publicly at the UN in October 1965,' according to then-High Commissioner MacDonald, as quoted by Michael Hilton in an unpublished thesis. 'However, at the OAU meeting in Dar es Salaam following UDI, Kenyatta

*Malcolm MacDonald, Kenya's British-appointed Governor at the time of independence*

## The 'Reluctant Politician'

gave him strict instructions to make no reference to the use of military force and to encourage the other governments to support the British.'[49] Hilton also quotes MacDonald as recalling being told by Njonjo that 'whenever anyone like Murumbi had suggested military force [against Rhodesia] in Kenyan cabinet discussions during the last eighteen months Kenyatta had countered the suggestion'.[50] On the matter of South Africa, which proclaimed itself a bulwark against communism, Murumbi speaks in his reminiscences of his opposition to South Africa's apartheid policies. 'To negate human freedom and liberty...is wrong in America and is wrong in the Soviet Union, is wrong in South Africa, it's wrong everywhere, wherever it occurs,' he says. There is some evidence, however, that over the years Murumbi toned down his earlier outspokenness, and that he, along with Kenyatta, Njonjo and others, felt that economic considerations were too great to allow for more militancy.

In 1967, after Murumbi was out of politics, MacDonald told the Colonial Office that Murumbi and his former Government colleagues had considerable sympathy with Malawian President Kamuzu Banda's policy of maintaining good relations with South Africa, 'though they criticize the methods which he sometimes uses to pursue it'. MacDonald added that Murumbi had told him a few weeks prior 'that all the African leaders must come to recognize that Banda's policy is realistic and makes sense'. Then, he added parenthetically, 'His view is no doubt coloured by the fact that he is now a local head of Rothman's tobacco company with important business connections with South Africa; nevertheless, his influence is quite significant in various black African countries where he travels.'[51]

Whatever their differences, Kenyatta continued to rely on Murumbi, and Murumbi, in turn, remained loyal to Kenyatta throughout the shift to one-party government and the ruthlessly enacted Constitutional changes that effectively pushed Odinga and his supporters out of government. Even on the matter of Rhodesia, Murumbi, by his own description, ultimately bowed to Kenyatta's wishes. Recalling one particular situation, he said: 'I threatened to resign, or rather offered my resignation; he took me into the garden at State House and said, "Now, let's agree to differ, but I don't want you to resign."'

## Tough on Asians

One subject on which Murumbi was absolutely firm was the need for Kenyans of Asian descent to declare their loyalty to their adopted land. This was despite the fact that he and others had so often obtained help from Asian Kenyans during the independence struggle, and raises the possibility that, in those early years, he felt a need to dispel any possible questions about his loyalties. In a 1963 interview with an India-based news service, Murumbi described the Indian community in Kenya as having, with a few exceptions, 'sat on the fence' as he put it, during the independence struggle. Commenting on the fact that the new Government of Kenya had accepted the resignations of 2,000 Indian civil servants who had been part of the East African Common Services Organisation, Murumbi claimed: 'Indians tried to take advantage of what they thought was our African vulnerability. They expected we would give in to their demands. We can do without them.' He added, 'I think this incident proves that they are not really citizens of this country, they have no interest in this country.' [52]

In similarly tough remarks in a 1965 letter to an Indian friend in Madras, Murumbi wrote that more than three-fourths of the Indians living in Kenya had registered with the British High Commission as British subjects, and many Indian businessmen were sending their money to the UK. 'The feeling is growing among our people that if the Indians have no confidence in Kenya they should not be allowed to reside here and this feeling may well have very serious consequences in the future,' he wrote. [53]

*The 'Reluctant Politician'*

## No Money, No Land

Given his frequently expressed sympathy for former Mau Mau fighters, it is somewhat surprising that Murumbi went along with the Kenyatta government's lack of assistance to them, and its refusal to consider expropriating European farms—a position supported by Bildad Kaggia, Oginga Odinga and many others—in order to give land to the landless. In the preface to *Mau Mau from Within*, which was published in 1966, Murumbi and three others including Kaggia jointly wrote that while Kenya's independence had come about 'largely because of this [Mau Mau] revolt,' too often the fighters' 'past and the movement they created is condemned by people of stature in the politics of the country today'.[54] But Murumbi raised no public outcry when, as Ndegwa coldly puts it, the Kenyatta government concluded that 'Financial compensation for the former Mau Mau, however attractive and humane it may have looked, was out of the question'.[55] Years later, Murumbi commented that 'free land, free education—these things are alright as propaganda stunts, but whether they are practical is another matter'. Kaggia himself, who had been in detention with Kenyatta, died in abject poverty.

Similarly, for all Murumbi's expressed admiration of Odinga, he went along not just with the decision to strip Odinga's power within KANU at the 1966 Limuru conference but also, after Odinga's subsequent resignation as Vice-President, to take over Odinga's role. When Odinga's Lumumba Institute, on whose board Murumbi sat, was shut down by the Government in 1965 after events including an Institute attack on Sessional Paper No. 10 (which Murumbi says 'I didn't agree with') he appears to have made no protest. The Paper was a blueprint for development which mentioned socialism but was clearly capitalist in outlook and favoured the already more advanced Central Province on the grounds that investment there would produce greater benefits.

On the matter of democratic government, Murumbi, who talks in his reminiscences of his belief in the need for opposition parties, made no protest when, in 1964, with the collapse of

KADU, Kenya effectively became a one-party state—a situation that was to continue for the rest of Murumbi's life. (To be fair, both scholars and politicians at the time made the argument that the best way to build national identity and stability in Africa was through single mass parties.)

What these actions of Murumbi suggest is that while he might have held personal opinions at variance with official ones, he was not a firebrand. Rather, for a considerable period of time he remained a loyal supporter of Kenyatta and KANU and was prepared to mute his disagreements and swallow his disappointments. This assessment of Murumbi was shared by the American CIA; in a 1965 biographic register entry, he is described as having 'tried to keep a foot in both the moderate and radical camps, but when the chips are down, he generally goes along with Kenyatta'. [56]

And even when he did decide to leave Government, he went quietly into retirement rather than making a public declaration of his differences. Indeed, when he learned while at a Commonwealth Prime Ministers meeting in London that the opposition led by Oginga Odinga was claiming that he would be joining them, he sent a telegram to Kenyatta in which he said, 'I wish to assure you, the party and the country that I have no, repeat no, intention of joining KPU and hereby wish to make it absolutely clear that my loyalty to you, to the party and to the country remains firm and unshaken and cannot be undermined'. [57]

## The Decision to Resign

In his reminiscences Murumbi suggests his resignation was the result of an accumulation of reasons and events. His health may have played a role (it appeared in a draft resignation letter but not in the final version); he had heart problems that twice in 1964 and 1965 forced him to take breaks from his duties.

A desire to earn more than he made in Government may also been a consideration: he talks in his letter about having 'my future to consider' [58] and elsewhere speaks of his hope 'that I may be able to show that it is not only in Government that a man can work for his country'. [59] In a profile in *Flamingo* magazine, he is quoted as saying, 'I feel I have done my bit in the political field.' [60]

But those who knew him point to two factors as having been key. The first was the murder of his close friend Pio Pinto. 'He was so disgusted that a young man like Pio Pinto was gunned down, a man who also worked locally among the Africans to bring independence to this country', William ole Ntimama, an important Maasai political leader, recalled in an interview for a 2010 TV series 'Makers of a Nation'.

Ntimama also cited the issue of growing corruption. In that same interview he said that Murumbi called him in 1966 and told him he was going to resign 'because I cannot be part of corruption in the country'. [61] Along the same lines, in a letter to his old friend Leslie Hale in January of 1967 in which he talked about his resignation, he wrote of his concern that 'things in Kenya are not going the way they should' and that 'we have thrown overboard all our socialist principles'. [62]

Nonetheless, he assured Hale, he and Kenyatta remained 'on the best of terms'.

Kenyatta's response to Murumbi's resignation letter, addressed to 'My dear Joe', was warm and affectionate. After praising Murumbi for his contribution in the struggle for independence, Kenyatta wrote, 'I have found you a wise and true counsellor and a warm and loyal friend,' and he ended by asserting his high regard for Murumbi 'as a person and a patriot'. [63]

Perhaps retired journalist Joe Kadhi gets closest to the truth when he says of Murumbi's resignation: 'I think he discovered that he was a square peg in a round hole.' [64]

**IN MURUMBI'S WORDS**

# The 'Reluctant Politician'

Mzee Kenyatta wanted me to take over the KANU party headquarters, which was on Jevanjee Street, and reorganize it, and also to be treasurer of the party, because we were going to have elections [in mid-1963.] I spent three days in the office seeing what was happening there and how the office was being run. And then I made a report to the Old Man. I said we'd need about £9000 [about £178,000, or Ksh 2.5 billion, in today's terms] because the rent was unpaid, the telephone was unpaid, the whole office was in disorder. I gave him my report and he asked me to see Mboya for money.

I saw both Odinga and Mboya and neither could provide the money. Odinga was the Vice-President and Mboya was the Secretary General of the party. So, I went back to the Old Man and I said, 'Neither Odinga nor Mboya can give me any money.' He said, 'You go and talk to them again.' So I did the rounds again, and neither of them had any money. (I think Mboya had the money, but he didn't want to help the party.) Then I wrote a letter to the Old Man I said, 'As the money is not forthcoming, please accept my resignation, and thank you very much for having confidence in me.'

Within an hour the Old Man was at my house in Nairobi South; I was not well that day. The first question he asked me was, 'Have you been to the press?' I said, 'For what reason? I have nothing to do with the press. You appointed me as treasurer and organizer of the party, and I'm sending you my resignation. It has nothing to do with the press.' So he argued with me and he said, 'Look here Joseph, I'll give you a thousand pounds.' I said, 'A thousand pounds is nothing. I can't do anything with a thousand pounds.'

He was afraid that I'd gone to the press. But I had no intention of going to the press. It was something between him and me, it had nothing to do with the press. So, we settled for two thousand pounds, and within a week I was to get another seven thousand pounds. I said, 'If I don't get the money, you'll get another letter of resignation.' After a week I got the other seven thousand pounds.

My task was now to reorganize the whole office. The first thing was to pay the rent. Then I paid the telephone bill, so we were in communication with the outside world. And then I called the staff and I said, 'Look here, I know you people haven't been paid your full salary and the amounts outstanding to you. I don't know what the amounts are because there are no books here'—because the previous treasurer used to draw the money in cash, pay them half salary, and pocket the rest of the money. I said, 'Now I want you to be honest with me, because if not you're not deceiving me, you're deceiving your own party.' I think everyone of the staff was honest enough to tell me the truth, and I knew exactly how much was outstanding to each one. I said, 'I'll pay you your outstanding salary in instalments that will be added to your cheque each month, together with your monthly salary.' And I said, 'You will get a cheque, not cash.' So, this way they were happy, they all had their money, and I think I paid everybody off in about three or four months.

And then I reorganized the interior of the office. I had an office for the President, I had an office for Odinga, I had an office for the Secretary General, Tom Mboya, and I had an office for myself. Mwai Kibaki [then a KANU official] was there and he came through one day and said, 'Joe, I've got a very small office.' I said, 'Come and look at my office.' My office happened to be a little bigger than his. I said, 'Now you take my office.' 'Oh no, no, Joe, I won't take your office.' I said, 'No, no, I insist, all I want is a little space where I can put a table and a chair, that's all I want to work. You have my office, please.' So we switched offices, and it satisfied him.

I had a typist pool, and I had a waiting room, because it was pandemonium in the office if visitors were around, looking about all over the place. So I had to get some discipline. I did get people to remain in the waiting room until they were called and seen by somebody. And everybody who came to the office had to be attended to and not wait for hours there and then have to go away without being seen by anybody.

Once I got the office into some working shape, the next thing was to begin to prepare for the elections. One of the most important things I thought was that we should have vehicles for our candidates. I remember P K Jani, who I think lost some money on this, used to get us second hand vehicles, Land Rovers, and we tried to get as many Land Rovers to our candidates as possible. We also had to have a proper election manifesto, setting out the aims and objectives of KANU. We roped in a journalist who used to work for *The Standard* and for a paper in London and we sat down and made a very fine election manifesto. It was more or less based on the British Labour Party's election manifesto.

We were able to get some money locally. I remember one candidate who used to come to the office and say, 'Is my money ready yet?' If I said, 'No', he would say, 'Look here, I can't waste my time, I've got to go and campaign.' So he'd rush off campaigning and come later on for his money. He was one of those good candidates who was bent upon doing a job, even without money.

## A Bagful of Cash

We found ourselves short of money for the [May 1963] election, so I told Mzee, 'Now if you give me letters of introduction to Algeria, Tunisia, and Kuwait, I'll bring you some money.' I went off armed with letters from Mzee. I was away for two weeks.

I went first to Algeria. Ben Bella was in power at the time. I was called up to his office and he told me, 'Mr Murumbi, I'm sorry I cannot spare any time with you because I've got to go to a funeral in the south of Algeria. But my friend here will look after you and will help you.' It so happened that I knew his friend very well because in London when I was working for the Moroccan Embassy I used to do all the work for the Algerians, who had an office in London,

## The 'Reluctant Politician'

just before Independence. He said, 'Joe, come and see me tomorrow morning.'

So I came the next morning. He had a huge pile of crisp bank notes—Algerian bank notes. I looked at it and said, 'What the hell am I going to do with new Algerian notes?' He said, 'Joe, we have no sterling, we have no dollars, we've only got Algerian money—take it or leave it.' So I was left with no alternative but to take it. It amounted to about £9000. I went back to the hotel—I had one of these lockers in the hotel—and I asked the manager for the key and he came along and opened the locker for me, and I shoved all these notes in. He was looking at me and clearly wondering where the hell I got this money.

I had to think now about how I was going to change this money. My next stop was Tunisia. I was going to be going into Tunisia with a big bundle of these notes—they filled a whole airway bag. I went back to my friend, I said, 'Look, if I go into Tunisia with the money and the Customs examine my bag, they'll arrest me and think I pinched that money. The best thing for you to do is to call the Tunisian Ambassador in Algeria, tell him I have this money and tell him I'm going to Tunisia to see Habib Bourguiba—I've got a letter for Bourguiba from Mr Kenyatta to take me through Customs.' So all these arrangements were made.

A man from the Tunisian Foreign Office met me at the plane and I was taken through Customs and the Customs officer said, 'Any currency?' And the fellow said, 'No, VIP, VIP' and he pulled me through. They took me to my hotel and there was no locker in the hotel so what was I going to do? I had one of these little airways bags which you could cut open with a sharp knife or a razor blade—it was made of plastic material.

I was told Bourguiba was somewhere upcountry and he was coming back in a week's time. It was terrible to have this money and nowhere to keep it. I couldn't stay in the hotel all the time guarding this money, I had to go out, but always with that dreadful thought that somebody knew I was carrying a large amount of money and would kill me. Sometimes I used to risk it and put the money in my suitcase, go out, then rush back to the hotel and feel the suitcase...the money was still there. So anyway, nobody attacked me or robbed me.

A week later Bourguiba arrived in Tunis. There was a waiting room with a man sitting at the desk and there I was with this bag and there were some security men—they were all in plain clothes but I think they were security men – all watching me and that bag.

I felt rather uneasy because I knew what was going through their minds: that this man has got a bomb in there or a submachine gun or something, and he's going to kill the President. The time came for me to go in and see the President; I was flanked by two security men and led into Bourguiba's office. I said, 'Good morning Mr President, thank you very much for seeing me.

Before I say anything to you, Mr President, I must tell you what's in this bag because I think your people are rather worried.' I zipped open the bag and said, 'Mr President, I've got Algerian money here. There's no bomb in it.'

I explained to him how I'd got the money and he laughed like anything. He said, 'It reminds me of the old days when we were taking our independence.' He said, 'What do you want me to do?' I said, 'Mr President, I've come here because I can't change the money in Kenya; can you help me to change this money?' He said, 'All right. Now as regards your letter from Mzee Kenyatta, I'm giving you £5000.' I said, 'Can this money be paid by your Embassy in London into our bank account there?' He said, 'Ok, that's fine.' 'Now,' he said, 'With regard to this Algerian money, I'll have to call the Governor of the Central Bank and he'll give you exchange.'

The Governor of the Central Bank and I counted the money and I paid it into the Central Bank. The money had to go to Paris to be changed in Paris and then sent to London in sterling, then paid into our account, and we finally got it in Nairobi in time to help us in the elections.

Then I went from to Kuwait to see the Sultan. The Kuwaitis told me, 'Look here, our Embassy in London will pay you.' But they delayed and we got the money—£14,000—after the elections.

## Election Victory

The elections came finally and KANU won the election. I stood for Parliament, for Nairobi South, and I won the elections with a pretty good majority. It was a mixed area: European, Asian, and African.

Whilst Mzee was in London for the [final] constitutional conference [in late 1963] reports came back to us that the British Government was paying very little attention to our delegation, the KANU delegation. The settlers were fully backing KADU. People like Daniel arap Moi,

Masinde Muliro, and others were completely under the thumb of these white settlers. The settlers felt that there would be greater security under a KADU government than a government under President Kenyatta—that is, a KANU government. And to a certain extent they were supported by the British Government. We felt that any form of regional government, which KADU supported, would not promote unity.

I was then acting Prime Minister [in the pre-independence KANU government], so when I got these reports I called a Cabinet meeting and told my colleagues that we should take some immediate action to force the British Government to pay some attention to our delegation, to the KANU delegation. We decided that we would send a cable to Mzee in London telling him that we were going to declare UDI on the 20th of October. I sent telegrams to all our party branches, and had a tremendous response; they all said they were backing the delegation to the hilt.

The British Army was stationed in Kenya at the time. And instructions were given to arrest us all in case we went ahead with our plans for UDI. However, the tide had completely turned, and the British Government paid more attention to our delegation.

## A Fear of Regionalism

We knew the motive for the Europeans siding with KADU, and we knew also that to a certain extent the British Government was siding with KADU because they felt that KADU would protect the interests of the Europeans, although the Europeans had a very fair deal from the KANU Government. The Europeans felt that if they had a regional-style government there wouldn't be a very strong central government and they would be able to protect themselves against the central government. That was one factor. The second factor was, we felt that particularly after independence we needed nationalism. We felt that regionalism, any form of regional government, would not promote unity; it would also perpetuate, to a certain extent, tribalism.

We could have overcome that by limiting the powers of the regional assemblies and making the central Government a federal body and leaving some of the powers locally—for instance those involving development. Land would have been controlled by the local bodies. There wouldn't now be this fear of Kikuyu domination. We were influenced by the support of the Europeans for regionalism; we distrusted their ideas. But we were wrong because the Kikuyu took advantage of this. The subsequent developments whereby the Kikuyu exploited that situation came afterwards, when they realized that they would have control of the key ministries, the key appointments in the Government, the Provincial Commissioner. The civil service was completely in their hands.

Odinga, Tom Mboya, and others who were generally of the idea that we should have a unified government worked towards it, they supported it. But they began to see this discrimination. Those who spoke up were penalized. This eventually formed the break so that Luo leaders like Oneko and Odinga formed the Kenya People's Union. There were other non-Luos like Waiyaki and others who also supported it.

## 'Call me Malcolm'

The Governor the British Government appointed to carry on the transition to independence in Kenya was Malcolm MacDonald. He realized straight away that KADU was not the party to hand over to, under the influence of the settlers who were hoping that they would get KADU

*The 'Reluctant Politician'*

JOMO KENYATTA
FATHER OF OUR NATION

FOR COMPLETE INDEPENDENCE IN 1963

FOR PERSONAL FREEDOM AND SOCIAL JUSTICE

FOR ECONOMIC PROSPERITY AND SOCIAL SECURITY

FOR THE RIGHT OF WORKERS TO A LIVING FAMILY WAGE

FOR FREE EDUCATION FOR ALL OUR CHILDREN

FOR A NATIONAL HEALTH SERVICE

FOR A FREE AND UNITED AFRICA

KANU ELECTION SYMBOL - A COCK

into power. MacDonald saw through it and he's the one who told his Government, 'You're barking up the wrong tree.' And he's the one who switched the minds of his Government over to KANU and not to KADU.

He was a good administrator and it was a pity that we didn't have MacDonald earlier in Kenya's history.

When MacDonald came in at the start of 1963, State House was open, and we used to have parties, he invited us for dinner, for lunch and tea. I remember he sort of broke down the barrier between Europeans and Africans. He started off by setting an example. I remember when we were sworn in for the first Government, after I was sworn in he shook hands with me and said, 'Well, I hope you will call me Malcolm'.

But he was very cunning, he was always trying to get information out of you. He'd ring me up in the evening and say, 'Joe, I want to come and borrow a book.' He'd come to my house driving his Rolls Royce, with an open shirt, and sit down and talk. We sat talking politics. You know, it wasn't a book he wanted, he wanted the opportunity to talk. He was interested in art and I was interested in art and we both used to have a lot to talk about—what was happening in Kenya, and also we talked about art. And sometimes I was invited for tea to State House and that was just trying to get inside information. I was very careful with him.

## Foreign Affairs — Setting out the Philosophy

After the mid-1963 elections we were in the interim Government for six months before independence. I was appointed Minister of State. We had two Ministers of State. Mbiyu Koinange was one, and he dealt with African affairs, and I dealt with Foreign Affairs. After a year I was made Foreign Minister.

*Joseph Murumbi at a meeting at the UN with Fitz de Souza and Robert Ouko*

The day after independence, we were to go to New York for Kenya's admission to the United Nations. We had already appointed an Ambassador to the United States who also looked after the UN. That was Ambassador Burudi Nabwera. US Governor Stewart Udall represented the President of the United States at our independence celebrations and he flew out to Kenya on Air Force II. They were kind enough to give us a lift to New York in this plane. We flew from Nairobi to Rome and spent the night at the Hilton in Rome. We took off the next morning and refuelled at Shannon, arriving in New York where they dropped us off. Governor Udall proceeded on to Washington. We were very grateful for having the opportunity of flying on that beautiful plane. When we were at the UN we met UN Secretary General U Thant. Of course, there was the little ceremony of hoisting the Kenya flag as a member of the United Nations with U Thant in attendance.

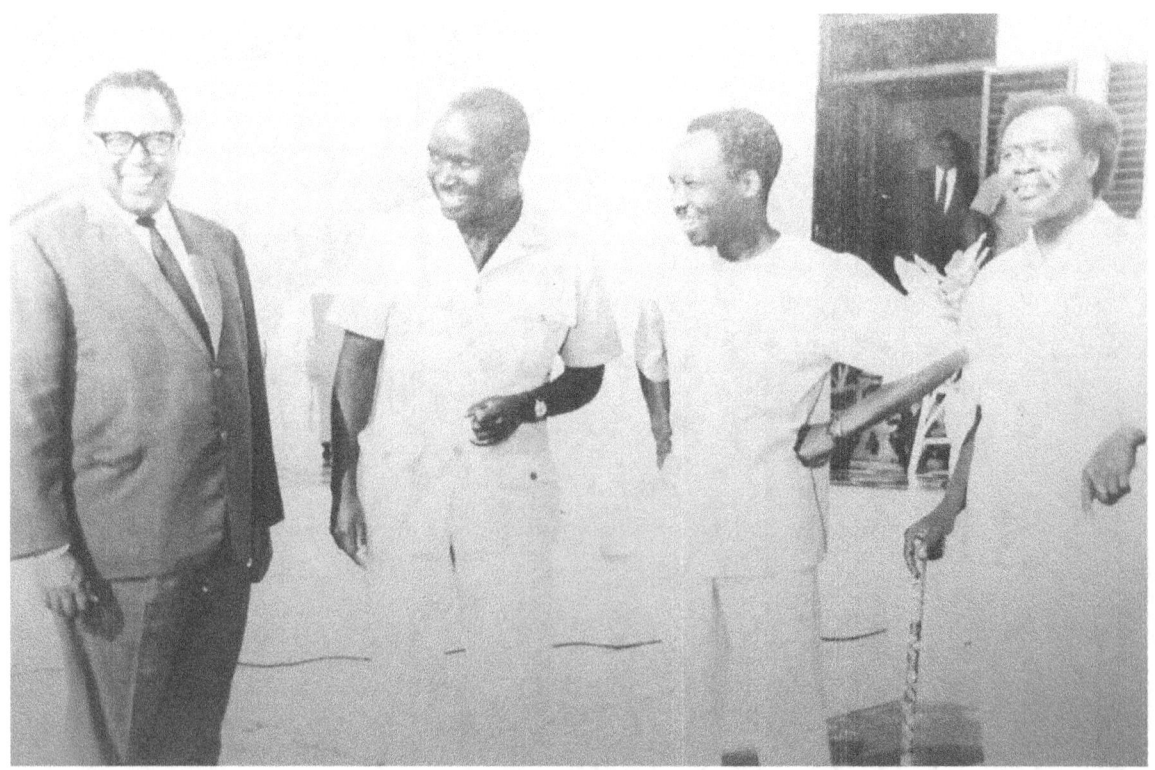

*Joseph Murumbi with Presidents Kenneth Kaunda of Zambia, Julius Nyerere of Tanzania and Milton Obote of Uganda*

We had the rare opportunity of meeting President Johnson who had come to New York for the General Assembly. He didn't say very much except, 'Oh, America wants to be friendly with Kenya.' We said, 'Yes, Mr President, we want to be very friendly with your country.'

The first impression of the United Nations was rather overwhelming. There's this enormous hall and all the delegates from different parts of the world. Being raw in politics it made a great impression on us. Later on, as Foreign Minister, after going to the United Nations every year, it became less overpowering.

Mzee used to ring me up and ask me what the newspapers were saying, and I had to get the papers so I was able to brief him. But, I don't think he was very much interested in foreign affairs. I think the point which I would like to emphasize is this: while I had a free hand in foreign affairs, I never exploited this in any way. I never would do that. And I think I could say that I never let him down. All along, the interest of the country was paramount to me; I always maintained that, and I never deviated from that in any way.

Whenever I had to attend either the United Nations General Assembly or a Non-Aligned Conference, or even the Commonwealth Prime Minister's Conference to which on two occasions I led the Kenya delegation, I always went to the President and said, 'This is the agenda for the meeting, this is the line I think we should take. If you disagree, tell me.' Invariably, he told me, 'Joe, you go ahead, I know you will do the right thing.' And I always had his support, except on only one occasion, which was Rhodesia. I also had the support of Parliament; if you look to *Hansard* [the official Government transcript] you will find very few questions were put to me on foreign affairs.

My principles, the principles which have guided me in foreign affairs, were first, the interest of Kenya was paramount. Secondly, we were members of the Organisation of African Unity, and therefore we should work closely with the OAU and more or less have our policies in foreign affairs in line with the OAU policies. Thirdly, we were members of the United Nations, and we should give the United Nations all our support. And lastly, we were a non-aligned country and therefore we should be able to choose our friends without dictation or interference from any country saying whom we should be friends with and whom we shouldn't be friends with. In other words, we should have a completely independent foreign policy which was not dominated by any country, any of the big powers—America, the Soviet Union, China, Britain, France or anybody. That guided me in my foreign policy.

At that time there was a strong feeling of Pan-Africanism. It was largely through the efforts of a few countries: Nkrumah of Ghana, Sekou Toure of Guinea, the President of Mali, Nasser, Ben

Bella, Kenyatta here in Kenya, Nyerere, Haile Selassie, Kenneth Kaunda. We formed a hard core in the OAU. We created the spirit of Pan-Africanism, a very strong feeling. We took united actions at times, supported each other, and we more or less dominated the OAU. Later on, things deteriorated, and the OAU is nothing like what it was in those days.

We were respected by the other African countries and we played our part in many of the events of that time. Everybody looked up to Kenya to have a progressive foreign policy, being a country that, like Algeria, fought for our independence.

I think Mboya was very disappointed that he was not appointed the first Foreign Minister. I think he had told people before independence that he was to be the first Foreign Minister, but he had nothing to do with foreign affairs. I think Mboya had, within the Cabinet, a few friends who would not attack me directly, but I used to feel pinpricks now and again, and I saw the hand of Mboya.

*Murumbi with Ghanaian friends at the All-African People's Conference in 1958*

*The 'Reluctant Politician'*

## 'Isms' and Aid

The sessional paper on African socialism was the brain child of Mboya. But Tom was by no stretch of imagination a socialist. He was a capitalist. I have always been at heart a socialist. But I don't believe there is any type of socialism called African Socialism. Socialism as a concept exists in various forms, the extreme form of which is communism or, in a milder form, that which is practiced by the British Labour Party or the Labour Party in Scandinavia. But there's no form of socialism ever conceived in Africa either today or in the past, or even before the advent of colonialism. What is more important is to establish democracy in the true sense of the word.

I don't think there is a clear understanding of the dangers of communism. There is no equality in a communist state, as people believe. People should realize that communism is a very rigid, monolithic system where you are subservient to the state, you are a cog in the political machine of the state, you cannot express an opinion contrary to the wishes of the state, there is no democracy.

James Gichuru was head of Treasury at the time, and he and Mboya were aligned. And, later on, I think they were influenced a lot by William Attwood because, at times, I knew from other sources that when I attacked the Americans, for instance, in the General Assembly or the Security Council, on Vietnam or American policy in the Congo, Attwood influenced people to say, 'Joe is making a mess of things. If he's going to attack the Americans, they will reconsider their aid policy to Kenya.'

Well, I think it's wrong to be influenced by somebody giving us aid, and threatening that they will withdraw this aid if you attack the policies of that government. You should have the freedom to do that. I remember that I used to have a discussion with Dean Rusk every year at the General Assembly for at least three quarters of an hour. I used to tell him, 'If I attack the American policy, it's because we in Kenya feel that your policy is wrong. But this does not mean that we are enemies of the United States. If we are friends of the United States, I think we should have the freedom to tell you to your face when we feel that your policies are wrong. Don't misinterpret that as being anti-American.'

But we couldn't follow the line of not accepting any aid from anybody. I don't think any African countries have the resources to stand on their own and say, 'No, we reject this aid.' We either had to accept that aid or have chaos. And to us at that time it was advisable to accept the aid, although it had certain strings. But the point then is how you utilize this aid to become economically self-sufficient. And it's impossible to expect an African country, whose economy has been geared to a metropolitan country or to other European countries, within ten years or fifteen years to be able to be self-sufficient and to be independent and to be able to not accept any aid but instead to generate development funds from within. Those who criticized us are, today, in a worse position than we are.

Attwood is a peculiar character. He had a kink in his mind about the communists. Everybody who did not agree with him was a communist. He probably thought I was a communist as well, and the whole theme of his book *The Reds and the Blacks* is that he succeeded in keeping the communists out of Guinea and out of Kenya. When that book was published it annoyed many people in Kenya because many of our Ministers had confided in him and had talks with him and he revealed some of these talks. He annoyed people so much in Kenya that he was told quite clearly that he could not come to Kenya again.

Attwood played a role behind the scenes in a lot of things that have gone wrong in Kenya.

## Failure of Federation

The British program was for independence for Kenya in 1964 but we got it a year earlier in the hopes that we would then federate with Uganda and Tanzania. There would have been big advantages for East Africa. For example, we already had common services. And federation would have made East Africa a legal entity. Mboya, Koinange and I went to London to see Duncan Sandys, the Colonial Secretary, to ask him whether they would give us independence in 1963. Sandys said he'd put the matter to the Cabinet and let us know. And the British Cabinet agreed.

So when we got our independence we started negotiations with Tanzania and Uganda. Firstly, the three leaders, Mzee Kenyatta, Julius Nyerere, and Milton Obote, met in Nairobi and made a statement that they were going to study the question of federating, and representatives were nominated by the three countries to meet and discuss the whole issue. On the Kenya side were Mboya, Charles Njonjo and myself. On the Tanzanian side was Oscar Kambona.

We held our first meeting in Nairobi and subsequently we had a meeting in Dar-es-Salaam and a meeting in Kampala and we circulated in the three territories. After a while it became difficult to try to get any sense out of Uganda. The Ugandan representative was saying no to everything so we felt we'd reached a deadlock. And the result was that we felt that we could not pursue the matter any further.

We asked Mzee to call a meeting of the three heads of state. Milton Obote came out very clearly on the issue: he had difficulties which he hadn't foreseen when he said he was prepared to federate. He'd gone into the Constitution of Uganda and found that if the Uganda Government wished to federate then he would have to get the permission of the Kingdoms: Buganda, that means the Kabaka, and he was at loggerheads with the Kabaka; and from the Kings of Toro, Ankole and Bunyoro. He felt that in view of the antagonism of the Kabaka—he didn't say that but it was assumed that the Kabaka was the main stumbling block—he didn't think that he would get permission from the Kingdoms. Therefore, he was in a difficult position. Subsequently when the Kabaka was deposed, Obote said, 'Now I am ready for federation,' but it was too late.

Besides federation, we also had regional talks on defence. I was trying to get Uganda and Tanzania to discuss the question of having an East African force, but in order to have that we would have to standardize training and weapons, and have the Air Force training in one territory, the Navy in one territory and the Army in one territory. The officers would know each other and if there was a question of defending ourselves against attack from outside, there would be no confusion as when each army had different weapons.

While we were talking about this we came to know that Tanzania was negotiating with the Canadians to set up their Air Force while Uganda was negotiating with the Israelis to set up their Air Force and their Army. So behind our backs, while we were talking about standardization of our armed forces, they were making their own arrangements. So we dropped the idea and there were jealousies and rivalries because they wouldn't allow open travel among the territories.

## Post-Independence Crisis: Zanzibar and Lanet

Early one morning [in January 1964] at about two o'clock, I had a phone call from Prime Minister Shamti of Zanzibar informing me that there was a revolution there and requesting Mzee to send troops to assist the Government. I immediately rang Duncan Ndegwa, who was our Permanent Secretary, and asked him to meet me in the office as something urgent had cropped up. When Duncan came to the office, I told him the facts as I had heard them from Shamti in Zanzibar, and I proposed that we should contact Mzee. I didn't know where Mzee was, but Duncan knew that Mzee was somewhere in Kitale.

When we succeeded in contacting Mzee on the phone, he said that he had a few Ministers with him. They would hold a Cabinet meeting and let me know what we should do. In the meantime, I was to inform Obote and Nyerere and keep them posted of the situation as it developed. Neither Obote nor Nyerere—Nyerere in particular—had any clue that there was a revolution in Zanzibar. Obote was easily accessible by ringing Kampala or Entebbe. I told him the facts. However, it is very difficult to get hold of Nyerere after nine o'clock; all phone communications to State House are cut off. So I had to ring Oscar Kambona, who was then Minister of Foreign Affairs, tell him the facts, and ask him to get in touch with Nyerere to tell him what had happened.

This incident led me to remain in the office for three days, day and night, without going home. I was in communication with Shamti and informed him that Mzee had the message and he could expect a reply at any time. I was to ring Shamti at about six o'clock in the morning. I didn't get him, but I got his Permanent Secretary, who was an Indian, and I told him that I still hadn't received a reply from Mzee. I also asked him who was creating this trouble. Was it Karume? Surprisingly, he told me that two days before, Karume had warned there was going to be trouble, and the night before Karume had left for Dar es Salaam with his family in a dhow. So it wasn't Karume who was creating the trouble.

A little later I got a telephone call from our Commissioner of Police to the effect that with the help of the RAF, he had a plane ready at Nairobi Airport with a detachment of the General Service Unit [the police paramilitary unit] ready to fly off to Zanzibar. I asked him under whose authority he had requested a plane and under whose authority he was sending the GSU to Zanzibar. I told him that on no account should a single policeman or soldier or GSU be moved to Zanzibar without the authority of the Government. Moreover, the GSU should go back to barracks immediately, and if Mzee came to know about this he would be sacked.

The GSU returned to barracks. I had no information from Mzee, and there were repeated requests from Shamti for help. But after about eight o'clock in the morning I had no further communications from Zanzibar. Mzee came back to Nairobi at four o'clock, and we heard on the radio that by seven o'clock in the evening the revolution was over. The only fighting that had taken place, and was continuing to take place, was at the police station on the East Coast, but Zanzibar Town was in the hands of the revolutionary forces.

Much later on we came to know the whole story. John Okello [a Ugandan working in Zanzibar at the time of the revolution] was in Nairobi and Nyerere was here as well. Okello was invited to Mzee's office. Present were Nyerere, Mzee, Okello, and myself. We asked Okello what had really happened, what had sparked off the revolution. As we knew, Okello had played a very important part in it. Well, the story according to Okello was that a number of police officers from Kenya and Uganda were dismissed by the Zanzibar Government, which refused to pay their fares back to their own countries. Okello happened to meet some of these officers in a bar in Zanzibar, and they were complaining that they had received their salaries but hadn't been given their passages back home. So Okello said, 'Let's do something about it.'

Okello and the officers got together and they decided that they were going to take over Zanzibar. The plan was that these police officers should go to the police [barracks] one night and, being known to their friends, as they were ex-police officers, they would stay there. According to the African traditional custom of hospitality these people probably had a meal, they chatted, and as the night grew late they were told by their hosts, "Why don't you sleep here?" The plan was that they should get up about one o'clock in the morning, go together to the Zanzibar police station, and take it over as the first step.

They did this. Having taken over the police station, they opened the armouries. Okello had his men ready. Arms were distributed to them, and they attacked the mobile police unit in Zanzibar, which was taken over in a matter of an hour or two. In the confusion the Sultan boarded a ship and got away. The only resistance was the police station on the East Coast. By eleven o'clock in the morning, Okello and his gang realized that they had complete control of Zanzibar Island. They were confused as to the next step and didn't know what to do. As I said previously, Karume was in Dar es Salaam and so was Abdulrahman Babu [Secretary of the Zanzibar Nationalist Party]. So the revolutionaries got on the wireless and pleaded for Babu and Karume to come back to Zanzibar. They did come back and Karume took over the Government.

Okello became an embarrassment to the Zanzibar Government. I think they made a final settlement with him, gave him some money, and told him to go back to Uganda to see his parents.

Later, I was due to go to Lagos for a conference and the day before I left, at about four o'clock, I had a message radioed from Mombasa saying that Okello was on board a plane heading for Nairobi. I immediately rushed to the railway station to tell Mzee, who was leaving for Mombasa. He instructed me to remain in Nairobi and for Mbiyu Koinange to go in my place. I was to handle Okello and see that he was out of Nairobi as soon as possible. Okello arrived and I had to declare him a *persona non grata* in Nairobi. He left for Uganda almost immediately.

[Okello's role in the Zanzibar revolution remains unclear; some believe that he was a committed revolutionary and others that he was only a minor figure in a political drama whose particulars remain in dispute.]

After the Zanzibar revolution the troops in Dar es Salaam rebelled. Nyerere went into hiding, and it was through the efforts of Oscar Kambona, who courageously faced the troops—and credit should be given to him for this—that the mutiny amongst the troops in Dar es Salaam was quelled.

I had suspicions that there would be a repetition of this in Kenya, and I told Mzee that we should be on our guard in case our troops did likewise and mutinied. Mzee wouldn't believe me; he said this could never happen in Kenya. I persisted and told him, 'Let us be prepared and make our contingency plans in case anything like this happens in Kenya.' Finally, after some

## The 'Reluctant Politician'

time, Mzee agreed to it and told me, 'Joe, you can go ahead and do what you like.' I called the Commissioner of Police, the British Commander of the Army—that's the British Army which was in Kenya at the time—and the Commander of our own Army. We planned that in case there was a mutiny or any disturbance in the Army we would take very firm action to quell the rebellion.

It did happen in Kenya, the Army at Lanet mutinied [during the last week in January]. Fortunately for us we had a British regiment at Lanet and I'd arranged for advance permission to use British troops in case we needed them. Under normal circumstances it would have taken about eleven hours before the High Commissioner communicated the request to London and London replied with permission. In an emergency of this kind it was necessary to act immediately, so permission had been granted by the British Government for us to use British troops on application through the British High Commissioner, who at the time was Sir Malcolm MacDonald.

When the mutiny broke out at Lanet the British troops were nearby. As soon as the British Commander heard the shooting he got British troops to surround the Kenya Army camp. The result was that one civilian was hit by a stray bullet, one askari was killed, and four got out of the camp with two rifles and two revolvers. They were rounded up the next day. This saved a nasty situation because if the African troops had got out of the barracks armed, they could have created havoc in Nakuru, and of course this could have spread to other parts of the country. On this occasion also, I remained in the office day and night and we kept an hourly watch over the Langata barracks where there are Kenya Army troops. I also got hourly reports of the situation with the troops at Nanyuki. The mutiny did not spread any further, and therefore we saved a very nasty situation in Nairobi.

The ring leaders of the mutiny were court marshalled and some of them were imprisoned.

## The Soviet Union-China Trip

The Cabinet decided [in April 1964] that we would send a delegation to the Soviet Union. The purpose of this delegation was first of all to understand the Russians, and also to try to get economic aid, military aid and scholarships. Odinga, who was then Vice President, led the delegation and the other members of the delegation were myself and some other Ministers. We left for Cairo first and from Cairo we took an Aeroflot plane to Moscow. It was in May, I think, and I had no warm clothing at all except a woollen suit, but no overcoat, because from my experience in London in May it's not so cold. But when we arrived in Moscow Airport there were about two feet of snow on the ground. We had to go to an official reception where we were met by First Deputy Premier Alexei Kosygin and other Soviet officials. I was shivering like anything. They rushed me straight into the airport building, and after the ceremonies were over we were taken to our hotel. When I arrived at the hotel, there were about six long coats ready for me to try on. I selected a coat, which I still have.

The first talks we had were with Premier Nikita Khrushchev. I had seen photographs of Khrushchev, but found that he was a very small man, practically bald. In these meetings in the Soviet Union there is always a long table with glasses of mineral water and cigarettes, each delegation sitting across from one other. There were the usual speeches of welcome by Khrushchev and a reply from the leader of the delegation. We had taken some presents for Khrushchev. There was a *panga* and a homemade gun used by the Mau Mau fighters. He was very tickled with this, seeing the homemade gun as compared to the modern guns they have in Russia and in the Western world.

Odinga said that we were friends of the Soviet Union, and we'd come to see whether we could get some economic aid. Odinga wanted a hospital in Kisumu. We wanted some arms, and we wanted scholarships. And then Khrushchev said, 'Well, we'll study these questions,' and said they would give us a reply and put us in touch with various officials and we would then discuss matters in detail. Khrushchev went into a long tirade about the Chinese and how the Russians had helped them and how ungrateful they were.

On another occasion we had talks with Kosygin. I raised the question of Russian arms being supplied to Somalia which the Somalis were using against us. They were arming the *shifta*, who were fighting us in the Northern Frontier District. And Kosygin said, 'Well, who are you to ask us to whom we should give arms?' I got a bit annoyed with that and I said, 'We have come here as friends and surely you are not going to arm people who are fighting against us. If that's your attitude I think we may as well pack up and go home.'

I stood up to go out of the room. Odinga caught me by the coat and pulled me down. So I didn't say anything further. The next day Jacob Malik [a top Soviet diplomat] referred to this incident and said, 'As a matter of fact, we have taken steps already about this. Khrushchev has written a letter to the Somali President telling him that the arms they supplied were for self-defence and not to be used against any Somali neighbours, either Ethiopia or Kenya.'

To me, it seemed a very peculiar letter, it was on a narrow strip of paper and written by hand. They read it out—it was in Russian but they interpreted it. I said, 'May I have a copy of that letter?' They refused. They said, 'But we'll send a copy to our ambassador in Nairobi and he'll show it to Mr Kenyatta.' So I stayed quiet.

I remember one occasion, it was Lenin's birthday, and there was a dinner which was only for the members of the Presidium and our delegation, that is Odinga and myself and our Ambassador and I think one of our officials. After the dinner, there was to be a play on Lenin's life. In these Kremlin banquets, particularly with Khrushchev, you've got to knock back one vodka after another because there are so many toasts. Khrushchev used to drink very heavily. Odinga, of course, never used to drink; he used to just put that little glass to his mouth. I had to be careful myself because I couldn't keep up with Khrushchev. When dinner was over, Odinga was on Khrushchev's right hand, I was to his left. He put his hands through our hands and we walked along with him. And I could feel the weight because he needed some support because he couldn't walk straight. We actually supported him into the hall. So instead of sitting at the back of the hall in the row of seats that were reserved for us, we were made to sit on either side of Khrushchev right in the front.

We attended the May Day celebrations in Moscow. Whilst we were there watching the parade, Odinga was called up to be with Khrushchev and others on top of Lenin's tomb because that's the reviewing stand, on top of Lenin's tomb. I think Odinga must have been very highly elated to be there.

We also had talks with Marshal Rodion Malinovsky who was then Commander in Chief of the Soviet Armed Forces. He was a very nice man in the sense that he had a sense of humour, very jovial and a typical soldier. Odinga told him, 'Marshal, we have very many children in Kenya named after you.' And he replied, 'I'm not responsible for them.'

I'm sure the rooms in the hotel were bugged. I remember one of the members of our staff went for a walk around the block where this hotel was situated, and one of the Russians, I think security men, said, 'Where are you going?' He said, 'I'm going for a walk.' The man said, 'Come back to the hotel or you may get lost.' So he brought him back to the hotel. There was a dining room in the hotel but we were fed separately.

I had met a young Soviet economist at an economic conference in Moshi just after independence and he suddenly turned up at the hotel and said, 'Do you remember me?' I said, 'Oh yes, very well, we met in Moshi and you had dinner at my house.' And he said, 'Please can you come over to my house and have lunch? I've told my wife and family how you entertained me and we would like to return the invitation.' And I accepted.

On the day that I was to have lunch I asked the Soviet people who were looking after us in the hotel to give me a car. They asked me why I wanted the car. I said, 'This friend of mine, this gentleman, has invited me for lunch.' 'Oh,' they said, 'You can't go for lunch, we can't give you a car.' I said, 'Well he's invited me and I entertained him in Nairobi and he's interested in returning the invitation.' They were adamant that they wouldn't give me a car. Of course, I know the reason: I was the guest of the Soviet Government and protocol-wise I should have informed them that I had this invitation, which I didn't do, and so it was my fault. I didn't want to pursue the matter because if I had, I'm sure this man would have got into trouble—the KGB would have interrogated him, asked how he became friendly with me and what we discussed—so I dropped the matter.

I always found myself sitting next to Anastas Mikoyan [at the time First Deputy Chairman of the Soviet Council of Ministers] who spoke English very well, and is a remarkable man in the sense that he has survived so many regimes in the Soviet Union. I think he died recently and I think he died peacefully in his bed, not in a concentration camp in Russia or tortured by the KGB. When we were leaving Moscow, a man came to me and gave me a package, and I felt there were some bottles in that package. He said that this was with the compliments of Mikoyan; he was very sorry he couldn't come and see you off at the airport as he was leaving from another airport in Moscow for Tokyo for an economic conference. It was a very nice gesture of Mikoyan to send this champagne to me when I was going away. I like the Russian champagnes better

## The 'Reluctant Politician'

than I do the French ones.

After our talks, the Russians gave us a plane to take us to Peking. We had talks with Chairman Chou En-Lai who was a brilliant man. He did his homework before he met us and asked us some very pointed questions. With Chairman Chou En-Lai was Marshal Chen Yee who, like Marshal Malinovsky in Russia, was a soldier. I think he went through the World War with Mao Tse-Tung when he fought and ousted Chiang Kai Shek. He was a typical soldier and he was Deputy Foreign Minister, but a man whom you could talk to openly. He had a great sense of humour, and we got on very well with him. We had to fly to Shanghai to see Mao Tse-Tung and Marshal Chen Yee accompanied us. Talking on the plane, Marshal Chen Yee said a very remarkable thing: 'You know the Americans are strong, they have got atom bombs, hydrogen bombs. We don't care, they can even hydrogen bomb us, kill about three-hundred-million

*Joseph Murumbi and Oginga Odinga visiting Russia*

Chinese, and we'd be better off after that.' It showed the callous nature of Communists who have no value for human life.

Old Marshal Chen Yee and I became very friendly and he used to send me presents. I still have a beautiful silk embroidery of a horse. He sent me a small silk screen with embroidered birds on it, a beautiful thing.

So anyway, we arrived in Shanghai and we were taken to see Mao Tse-Tung who at that time was a sick man. As a matter of fact, he had to be supported by two nurses when he walked. He sat down and we had a few words—we were told that we couldn't be very long—so we spent about ten minutes with him just exchanging courtesies, we didn't discuss any politics.

The factories in China are not cemented or plastered outside. They look very crude and rough, but inside they're spotlessly clean and they have the most modern machinery. The

*Joseph Murumbi's China visit with Oginga Odinga*

Chinese are very hard-working people. No ground is wasted. They plant wheat almost to the tarmac of the road, and gardens are planted with wheat because the Chinese have got this enormous problem to feed millions and millions of people, so they can't afford to lose any space.

On the whole, the talks we had in China didn't amount to anything. They didn't give us any aid, but they were very courteous.

It was a long flight back to Moscow, so we had breakfast early in the morning in Peking. When we arrived at Minsk, I think, we were met by a Soviet official who said, 'Come and have light refreshments.' We thought just a cup of tea or coffee or something. We went there and we found a huge spread—cold meats, steaks, rice—and we couldn't refuse. The next stop was at Kutz. There again, they said, 'Come and have some light refreshments.' There was another big spread. As we were going on, it was getting towards midday, but it was breakfast time in those parts. So this was the third breakfast that we had had that day. Then by the time we got to Moscow it was lunch time, and they said, 'Come and have some lunch now.' I said we already have had three breakfasts today, we can't have another meal.

Thereafter, we had further talks with the Russians. They agreed to give us some arms. They agreed to build a hospital.

When we returned to Nairobi, after a few weeks we were invited by the Russian Embassy to see a film of our visit to Russia. It was a 35mm film on two reels. It was rather boring. I was very tired that day, I had had a heavy meal, and the chairs were nice and comfortable. During the film I started snoring, to the embarrassment of everybody.

## Somalia and the Congo Crisis

I have had long experience with Somalia, having served there during the British Military Administration and two years after the Administration, and so I know most of the characters in

Somalia and the politicians.

After Somalia became independent [in 1960], they had designs for a Greater Somalia. Now this concept of Greater Somali did not come from the Somalis; it's an idea which was developed by the British Labour Government. After the war, Britain intended to join the Ogaden with Somalia and British Somalia and also attach to that certain parts of the Northern Frontier District of Kenya.

This idea was taken up by the Somali Government and they were determined to unify these countries. And that would be Greater Somalia. The reason why they started the campaign against Kenya was that we have Somalis in the Northern Frontier of Kenya, but these Somalis are not indigenous to that area. The presence of Somalis is due to the fact that years ago, the Government of British Somaliland had deported, or exiled, some Somalis from there into the Northern Frontier of Kenya, and they formed the first settlement of Somalis there and gradually it expanded.

When the OAU was formed, there was a clause in the charter of the OAU that all African countries should accept the boundaries as they were at the time of independence. That was specifically put in because Africa was carved up irrespective of ethnic boundaries and if we hadn't put that clause in, there would have been claims and counter claims and the whole model of Africa would have had to be redrawn. Somalia did not adhere to this clause in the charter.

We were adamant that we were not going to give up an inch of our territory. The British turned round to the Somalis and said, 'Well, now it's a matter between you two people to settle.' But they did finally get the two sides together, Kenya and Somalia, at a conference in Rome. MacDonald was the Governor of Kenya at the time, and travelled with us to Rome. We had a conference, and we would not give way and we made our position clear: there's no point in talking about this because you have no claim on this territory and we're not giving up an inch of our territory. The conference, of course, was a failure.

An interesting side light of this Rome meeting was that I'm not a good air traveller and that night on the flight to Rome I did not sleep very well. The day we arrived in Rome we were invited to a Verdi opera, at an open-air theatre in Rome. I was very, very tired, very exhausted, and I couldn't stay awake. I dozed off and suddenly when there was a pause in the music, I let out a very loud snore.

A minute or two after, the lights came on. People started looking around at me—the acoustics of that place are so good that practically everybody had heard my snore. I quickly got out of the theatre and stayed out until the lights were off and then came back to my seat. Malcolm MacDonald always refers to that incident and says, 'Joe, that break in the music occurred because Verdi could not find a suitable note and you have provided that note, and they must put a plaque on that seat saying, "Joe Murumbi produced that note missing in Verdi's opera."'

Anyway we had a good trip to Rome although the conference brought no results, at least to the Somali side.

The Congo issue had been always worrying the OAU, and not only the OAU but also East Africa: Kenya, Uganda and Tanzania. Julius Nyerere, Mzee Kenyatta and Milton Obote met at Mbale in Uganda together with Chrisophe Gbenye and Gaston Soumialot, the northern leaders of the Congo who were fighting against Moise Tshombe. We tried to get them to realize that if the war continued in the Congo, and particularly with the mercenaries who supported Tshombe, there would be terrible atrocities committed and a lot of bitterness and suffering among the people. We decided that we would meet them and suggest to them that they meet with Tshombe and try to settle their dispute. They were quite prepared to meet with Tshombe.

As a result of this meeting I made a representation to the OAU at their meeting in Addis Ababa that we should form an ad hoc committee and the chairman of this committee should be Jomo Kenyatta and the purpose of this committee was for the OAU, through the ad hoc committee, to try to achieve peace in the Congo. This suggestion was accepted: Mzee Kenyatta agreed to be chairman, and we had a series of meetings. The one in Nairobi was of particular significance because we decided that the best course would be to get the cooperation of the American Government, which had supported Tshombe, had brought him back to the Congo, and were providing him with arms.

At the meeting in Nairobi it was decided that the OAU ad hoc committee should send a delegation to Washington to meet the American president and impress upon him the need for a meeting between Tshombe and Gbenye and Soumialot. We had influence over Gbenye and Soumialot and they were prepared to meet with Tshombe. But Tshombe was rather reluctant and we thought that as the Americans had helped him to return to the Congo, he would concede to the Americans' request and meet with these people. I was to lead the delegation to Washington.

Mzee Kenyatta, who was chairing the meeting, asked me to ring the American Ambassador, Mr Attwood, and tell him about the idea of the OAU ad hoc committee and ask him to warn Washington about the arrival of this committee. I got on the phone and spoke to Mr Attwood and told him I would meet him after the meeting was finished. He was waiting for me in his office and I told him all the details of the meeting and what we had decided to do and the reasons for the delegation.

The next morning Mr Kenyatta called Attwood up and asked him to come to his office and he repeated to him what I'd told him the night before. I was leaving for Washington that evening.

When en route to Washington I always broke my journey in London. The next morning, I was about to catch a TWA plane at the airport but whilst I was waiting I got a call from the High Commissioner to say that there was an urgent message for me from President Kenyatta, which was transmitted through the American Embassy, and that an officer from the Embassy was on his way to the airport to see me with the message. I told him that the plane was about to leave in half an hour. He said, 'Don't worry about that, the American Embassy has delayed the plane for two hours so it will be all right.'

This officer from the American Embassy arrived with a telegram from President Kenyatta. I read the telegram and it was contrary to my brief given to me by the ad hoc committee. The officer asked me to get in touch with Soapy [G Mennon] Williams immediately and he would get him on the line. Soapy Williams, the American Secretary of State for African Affairs, said he was rather disturbed about this delegation coming to Washington as it was election time and it might disturb the American elections. I said it had nothing to do with the elections.

He said, 'What about the propaganda and the publicity that you'll make? Are you going to make a press statement?' I assured him I would not make a press statement either on my arrival in New York or in Washington. The press knew of my arrival but I refused to make any statements.

In Washington I collected my luggage and then the representative of the American Secretary of State's office handed me a letter which was an invitation to have dinner with Soapy Williams that night. He gave us a very good reception when we arrived there and he took me straight into his study and handed me a bit of paper and asked me to read it and sign it. I read the paper. It was a statement which I was supposed to have made, saying that I'd been to Washington, seen the American Government, had talks with them, had talks with Soapy Williams, and I was going home.

I said, 'Well, Soapy, I'm terribly sorry, but who do you think I am? I have not had talks with you, I've not had talks with the President, and I cannot sign this statement. It's not my statement.' He said, 'Well, haven't you had instructions from the President?' He was very annoyed about this.

What had obviously happened, I think, is that Attwood had gone again to Mr Kenyatta after I'd left for London and told him that he better send me instructions, clear instructions, and the quickest way of getting the instructions to me in London would be through the American Embassy. Well, I didn't know why the Old Man consented to do this because normally any messages to me from my Government would be transmitted to me through our High Commissioner in London and not through the American Embassy. So obviously that message, which I say quite deliberately was distorted by William Attwood, and a copy sent to Washington, is why Soapy Williams told me, 'Haven't you had any instructions from your President?'

So we had dinner. It was a big roast. It was a hot roast but the atmosphere at the dinner was very cold.

The next day the other delegations arrived and we had talks with Soapy Williams. These talks continued for four days. It took us four days to convince them that we were sincere in our approach towards the problem, that we really wanted peace in the Congo, and all we were asking for was the cooperation of the American Government to try to get Tshombe, over whom they had influence, to join in the talks so that we could find a settlement and therefore achieve peace in the Congo and also get the mercenaries out of the country. We had lunch with Dean Rusk, a working lunch, and it was agreed that the American Government would help, and except for about two words which were altered in the communiqué, it was passed and signed. We went back to Nairobi and I reported to my President and at the next OAU meeting I reported the facts to the group in the OAU.

This crisis was important to us in Africa for various reasons. One, the fighting was being prolonged and, two, it involved mercenaries, foreign mercenaries, which was a bad thing for the future of Africa because the idea of Africans importing mercenaries to fight against other Africans, and the stories we heard about the activities of the mercenaries, presented a very sad, sad picture. Tshombe had the assistance of the mercenaries and the assistance of the American Government and also the Belgian Government. We did not approach the Belgians at all. But we thought that the Americans were the most important element in this situation. We were very disappointed because, although the American Government agreed to try to influence Tshombe, they didn't have any effect, and that is why we decided to pour arms into the Northern Congo to Gbenye and Soumialot.

[Internal fighting in the Congo ended when Joseph Mobutu staged a coup d'état in 1965 and became the country's leader.]

## Pio Gama Pinto's Assassination

February the 24th 1965 will always stand out in my memory as a sad day when I lost a very sincere friend. Both Sheila and I were very much affected by Pio's death, and every year on that day we visit Pio's grave with a bouquet of flowers to make him know that we still remember him. There are others too—I don't know who they are—who on the many occasions when I've been to his grave on the 24th of February have put flowers there.

I was at home having a shave when Achieng Oneko rang to say he had information that Pio had been beaten up at his home and I should go up and see what had happened. As I was not ready yet, I sent my driver and a man called Cheche who worked for me and said I would follow. I immediately dressed and rushed up to the house and parked my car beside Pio's gate. Pio's car was parked just a little outside the gate, and I saw Pio in there and I thought he was hurt. I rushed to him and I said, 'Pio what has happened, what has happened?' And the police officer told me, 'Don't say anything to him, he is dead.' It was a tremendous shock. His wife was in the office—she used to work for Achieng Oneko—so we sent for his wife, and news soon got around that Pio was dead.

The whole day we had people coming to the house. They were poor people, friends of Pio, people he had helped, people who had been with him in detention, and the place was jammed the whole day. The next day we buried Pio. People from far and wide came to the funeral, a requiem Mass. Pio was buried in the City Park, the main cemetery, and that was jammed with people.

There were many Foreign Ministers from the neighbouring territories like Oscar Kambono, Sam Udaka, and others who were in Nairobi at the time. They all came to the funeral. It was really pathetic to see elderly Kikuyu weeping their hearts out for a man they loved and respected, for a man who helped them in need, a man who was their colleague in detention, and a man who had never forgotten them.

*Pio Gama Pinto raised shoulder-high upon his election as MP*

Pio always worked for other people, he never worked for himself. He was always writing petitions, memoranda for Members of Parliament, helping people out of their problems, trying to find money to assist them, going to see the families of people who were away from Kenya on some job or the other. I remember when as Foreign Minister I was out of the country, he used to visit my wife Sheila and ask her whether she needed money, or he would take her out for a meal and make her feel comfortable whilst I was away. He did this for many people and when people were sick in hospital, he would visit them.

He was a man who never did any harm to anybody. As a matter of fact, he helped everybody from the President downwards. When I was looking after the Old Man's office and the press, and Pinto was also in the press, both of us were getting fifty pounds a month. He used to tell his wife his salary was twenty-five pounds, and that extra twenty-five pounds was handed out to people who had come out of detention, had no money, had no job. Every week Pinto would make up a list of people: two hundred shillings for so and so, a hundred shillings for somebody, fifty shillings for somebody.

I would never accept that Pinto was aiding the communists or was a communist himself. It was not a just accusation. I know Pinto had no contact with the communists at all.

Even today people speak with respect whenever the name of Pio Pinto is mentioned.

*Investigations at the scene where Pio Gama Pinto was shot dead outside his residence*

*The 'Reluctant Politician'*

## Dealing with 'Enemies'

There was no necessity for the murders of J M Kariuki [the MP killed in 1975], Tom Mboya [killed in 1969] and Pio [Pinto killed in 1965]. I think that particularly in the case of Mboya and Kariuki it was because they had political ambitions. I think they represented a threat to the interests in the establishment.

Well, let people have political ambitions. There's nothing wrong with political ambitions. Every man must have ambitions to rise, to achieve the highest position he can. But the interpretation is that these people may be a threat to the position of others and therefore they have to be eliminated. That type of attitude towards those who may pose a threat will cause people to resort to violence.

I don't know whether Mboya's murder was planned, I cannot say that with any certainty at all, but the fact that he was murdered is wrong. That's not the way to eliminate the opposition, by the bullet, and Mboya has played his part in Kenya politics, and very efficiently and very well. The fact that he was a very ambitious man is another point.

Kariuki is in the same category, but, in some cases, you see, people develop policies and tactics which put them into trouble, and Kariuki was too big-mouthed. He used to say all sorts of things, little realizing that he'd upset a lot of people.

There's a leader in power, but behind him there are a lot of other people who have their own interests and it may be this group that have engineered these things. People who are holding power want to hold on to power. You see the picture all over Africa—people who are threats are eliminated, thrown out of the job, thrown into prison, tortured or killed.

One of the things I can't be is a hypocrite. I've got to speak my mind out on these things, they are facts which everybody knows have happened, but nobody is courageous enough to say it. You can't distort history and sweep it under the carpet and pretend it's not there.

If a government is strong, and a government has the popular support of the people, then the

Dear Friends,

We have come here today to pay a final tribute to our dear friend and brother, Pio Gama Pinto, whose body lies before us, slain by brutal and cowardly murderers.

There is not one of us who has known this man and not benefited in some way from that knowledge. In life he made many sacrifices for his country, his party, and his fellow men. He has now made the supreme sacrifice and we can but hope that this senseless waste of a young and brilliant life will at least shock the whole country into realising that the bullet is no answer to any problem - it is an evasion. We must all follow the example set by our President, Mzee Jomo Kenyatta, and ensure that no bitterness clouds our emotions. This was one of the first principles followed by Pio Pinto himself. He suffered greatly in the cause of freedom, but never allowed himself to become embittered and never advocated the use of violence. Let us all vow, in his memory, that the rule of the mob, of unbridled crime, shall never be let loose in Kenya. Let us go forward together to create a peaceful united Kenya which will serve as a memorial to this great patriot.

I have known Pio, as so many of you have, for very many years and words cannot express the debt I owe to him for his never-failing friendship. He was a true man and a loyal man who never had a mean thought or performed a mean action in his whole life. The number of his friends gathered here today bears mute witness to this fact. He was everybody's friend and everybody was proud to know him.

To his wife, who shared his hardship and suffering, what can we say but to assure her that his memory will be with us always and that we will try to carry forward his cherished ideals and principles so that his beloved country of Kenya may flourish in peace and prosperity. To this very gallant lady I extend, on behalf of you all, the very deepest sympathy in her terrible loss and our assurance that the name of Pio Gama Pinto, freedom fighter and patriot, gentleman and Kenyan, will not be forgotten as long as we shall live.

*Joseph Murumbi's tribute to his dear friend Pio Gama Pinto* public will be content. But if they realize that the people they've elected are serving their own needs and are disregarding the purpose for which they were elected, which is to serve the people, well, in those circumstances you will get people individually dissatisfied, and if they have no means of redressing the situation through the ballot box, then they resort to violence.

If there is more than one political party then they have a choice not to resort to violence; they have the alternative of supporting a party which they feel would bring them justice, would work for their interests, and work for the advancement of the country. One of the most important aspects of democracy is to have the opportunity of an alternative government. I do not believe in the one-party state. Years ago, I wasn't for a second party. Now I am.

Being a Member of Parliament or being a Minister should not open the doors to wealth or power. You are elected a Member of Parliament, made a Minster, to serve your people. That is the essential fact which must be realized. If we do have more than one party, the excesses that are being committed in Africa under the guise of a one-party state will be eliminated.

## Asian and Mixed-Heritage Kenyans

One of the foremost Asians who tried to help us was Pio Pinto. There are others like Pranlal Sheth who was a lawyer, who was deported, wrongly in my opinion, and is now living in London, practicing in London, and is very happy there. Pran was a personal friend of mine, and also a very good friend of Mr Odinga; I think that's the reason why he was deported. Pran has been one hundred percent genuine. I would call him not an Indian but an African, just as Pinto was an African not an Asian.

During the trial of Kenyatta there were many Indians who helped us. There was Achhroo Kapila, there was Bashir Mauladad, P K Jani, Paul Assanand, Dave Gidoomal—they raised money for us at the time. Now those are people whom I feel have fully associated themselves with us. They all have interests in this country, and I wish there were more of them who would identify themselves and become fully integrated within Kenya. If they do, they can stay here as long as they live.

During the colonial times, except for a few individuals who sided with us, the Asians lent towards power, and that power was in the hands of the Europeans. But the Asians were not accepted fully by the Europeans either. I wish there were more Asians who would identify themselves and become fully integrated within Kenya.

You may see Indians and Africans going to a party together, but in their real social life they're as far apart as the poles.

When I was the Secretary of the Party [KAU] I was approached by people of mixed parentage and they asked, 'Would you become the chairman for a coloured people's society?' I refused. I said, 'Look here, you have either an African mother or an African father, in most cases it's an African mother. Invariably you are looked down on by people on your father's side. So why not sink in your lot with your mother's people and identify yourself with your mother's people?' They said, 'Well, would we be accepted?' I said, 'You will be accepted if you identify yourself as African. I'm accepted.'

## Arms

It was arranged with Odinga and the President [in 1964] that we would get some Soviet arms. The arms arrived by air and Odinga was to take delivery of them. Now Odinga had a man, one of his key fellows, called Rodney Miller. He put Rodney Miller in charge and had the airport sealed off when the planes arrived. The press happened to know about it and they wanted to know why the airport was sealed off. The arms were taken from the airport and in order to keep them in a safe place—it was done with the knowledge of the President—these arms were taken and put in a strong room in Odinga's office. Later on, we decided that they would have to go to the police armoury and we discussed it in cabinet. One night lorries came around and loaded the arms and took them away to the police armoury. There was never any intention that Odinga would use these arms against the Old Man. But it was misinterpreted by enemies of

Odinga—and he had a lot of enemies—that Odinga had these arms there and was going to use them against the Old Man.

We had another occasion where we had arms from Yugoslavia, and I told the Old Man, now let's handle this very carefully and avoid suspicions and false statements about it. They were coming by ship. I was entrusted with the handling of the whole operation. I called the General Manager of the shipping line and I said, 'Look here, this ship is coming with arms. I want plainclothes men looking after the ship. It must not be conspicuous, they must just be there watching everything. When the ship docks, I want some empty wagons alongside the ship. The arms will be offloaded straight away, put in these empty wagons, the wagons sealed, plainclothes men looking after this consignment, and these wagons hitched onto the first train going to Nairobi and it should be under plainclothes supervision.' And when they arrived at Nairobi they were taken from the railway station in a truck and deposited in the Yugoslav Embassy which is close to State House. There were plainclothes men, inconspicuous, watching this consignment until we could decide what to do with it. In this way, it appeared to be a consignment of stuff for the Yugoslav Embassy. A few days later we decided that these arms would be sent to State House and kept in the stores in State House under adequate protection and control. A few days later we sent them up to the police armoury and nobody knew anything about it.

During the trip to the Soviet Union led by Odinga, Odinga negotiated with the Russians a deal for the supply of arms. The Russians sent a shipment of arms [in 1965], which arrived in Mombasa, and the President sent me together with the commander of the British Forces in Kenya to inspect these arms. And what we saw was very disappointing; for instance, the T04 tanks, which were one of the best tanks at the end of the last war, were completely out of date. The tyres were worn and the turrets were damaged in some cases. The personnel carriers were old vehicles, painted up, with new tires. The machine guns were on tiny wooden wheels which were about a foot high, probably made between the First World War and the Second World War. On board, in charge of this contingent, was a Russian general. We knew from British Intelligence that he was a general, although he was in civilian clothes. I asked the general to produce the best rifle that he had out of this consignment. He opened up a case of rifles that were nicely greased, nicely packed in these wooden cases, and it was the best he could produce. I took a gun from one of our askaris, Kenya askaris—it was an FN rifle—and I showed it to the general and I said, 'Is your rifle as good as this FN rifle, you know this rifle very well?' He said, 'You're right. The FN is much better.' I said, 'What are you giving us?'

We decided that we had to report back to the President and the Cabinet. We told the President that we had rejected the whole supply of arms. They had already offloaded some personnel carriers and mortars and we called the Ambassador and told him, 'We don't want the arms, pack the ship with the arms you've offloaded and send the ship away.' Well there's no doubt about it, they offloaded these arms in Somalia, the same shipment. And subsequently, a year or two later, Malik, the Foreign Minister, was in Nairobi, on one of the occasions of our national days when we have our parade of our army, and I was talking to Malik and I said, 'You've seen our army, it's not sophisticated weapons which we possess, but it's modern weapons, better than the arms you sent us.' Malik agreed with me that we had more modern weapons. He said, 'Let's have a chat. We'll send you something better.' I said, 'No thank you.'

I know from experience the same thing has happened in many African countries. The Egyptians recently signed a contract with the British Government to repair the engines of the Soviet airplanes which they have now. Obote in Uganda had trouble getting spare parts for the Russian planes he had; he couldn't get tyres for the jeeps because the type is only manufactured in South Africa and the Soviet Union. I was in Uganda once, and the Minister of Défense said, 'Joe, try and get us some spare parts for those Russian jeeps and tyres', and he gave me a whole list and I said, 'Well, I'll speak to the Russian Trade Mission here in Nairobi.' I saw them and I gave them this list. I said, 'Can you supply these spare parts?' I got a reply nine months later, and for something I had never asked them for. If the Russians had wanted to, they could have sent Obote anything he wanted, flown out in big Russian transports, but relations had soured by that time.

I would say this as a warning to African countries: Try and get the proper relations with the Western countries and you can get the arms there on a much better footing than with the Russians. Because with the Russians, you've got to practically sell your liberty, or sell your crops as the Egyptians did with their dam that the Russians built; they had to pay for it in cotton. And I think even our friend Idi Amin [President of Uganda, 1971-79] has mortgaged some of his coffee and cotton to pay for some of the arms that he is getting from the Soviet Union or the satellite countries. So, it's a fallacy to believe that you can get arms very easily. You'll find yourself with arms from the Soviet countries, communist countries, particularly the Soviet Union, which after two or three years will be worth nothing more than the scrap value.

*The 'Reluctant Politician'*

## *The Eternal Problem - Land*

One of the problems we faced at independence was land. We were bombarded by people throughout the country shouting, 'We want more land, we want more land', because that was the central issue of our political struggle. There were areas in Kikuyuland where the people were all crowded, areas in Kakamega, in Luo land, where people hadn't enough land to live on. And one must remember that the British idea of creating reserves for each tribe was to make the reserves as small as possible so that all the people could not survive in the area, and there would be people without land, so that the European could thus get a constant supply of cheap labour.

With the coming of independence, the first demand was to relieve the land situation. We were in a dilemma, because our policy was not to confiscate land from the European. We appealed to the British Government for help and the British Government very kindly lent us the money to buy out settlers who wanted to leave the country, and we made no restrictions. It was done very fairly: the farmer named a price for his land, we had a government valuation of his land, and the African buyer was given a loan based upon the government value. If there was any difference in the price, the buyer had to supply it from his own pocket. Farmers who were bought out could take their money anywhere they wanted. In other words, we were receiving money from the British Government with one hand and we were paying it out on the other hand, and it was being taken out of the country.

The bigger farms were split up and made into settlement schemes. Unfortunately, at that time we didn't have a rural extension scheme so as to guide the farmers how to maintain these large farms which were taken over by settlement, with the result that these farms were split up into smallholdings. This is having a disastrous effect upon our economy inasmuch as these smaller units are only large enough to feed a family. In other words, they have lapsed back into subsistence farming, whereas the farm as a complete unit under one European was producing much more than these farms are producing today.

In the Thompson Falls area, where large ranches were taken over by settlement, the farmers were not able to meet their pre-payments to the AFC [Agricultural Finance Corporation] and they had to sell their stock. Therefore we have a shortage of beef in the country. Something has to be done about the productivity of these settlement schemes, they've got to be worked as one large unit with machinery, expertise, management provided, so that they can produce the maximum, and not be broken up into small units, because the whole idea of farming in Kenya should be not only to produce enough food for ourselves but to produce food for export.

If every inch of land in Kenya is properly managed, we will be in a position to feed ourselves and also to feed neighbouring countries. We must also remember that the world's population is increasing. Mankind is going to need food; he does not need coffee and tea, but he will need cereals, meat, etc. And a country which can produce food for export will be in a much better position in the long run than the Arab countries and the fabulous riches they are deriving from oil. Oil will dry up one day, but man has got to live. Man doesn't live by oil, man lives on his stomach, man has to eat, and the more food we can produce, the more we are helping mankind, and helping our own people, and if we can export, it will help us with our balance of payment problems as well.

There's another problem with the land because the settlement schemes are largely Kikuyu. The Kikuyu have spread out right up to Kitale and these areas are not Kikuyu tribal areas. The Kikuyu need land because they've been confined to a very small space and the population is rapidly increasing. But I feel that there must be a more equitable distribution of land, and not land reserved or given to one particular section of the people. There are other areas of land which are heavily overcrowded like in the Kakamega areas with a density maybe of about 5,000 to the square mile. There must be some relief given to the people. And areas that are still in Government hands should go to other tribes who badly need land. Now, unless this is solved fairly, reasonably and quickly, it'll amount to the same political situation which we were faced with vis-à-vis the European in colonial times: He grabbed all the best land and we hadn't enough land for our people. Now we have one section of the population grabbing land in Kenya because of certain opportunities which they have had and you are going to get a feeling of resentment which could result in political explosions down the road.

## Vice-President and then Out

When KANU had the Limuru Conference [in March 1966] it was quite clear that they were out to eliminate Odinga. Mboya was used by the Kikuyu to help with the elimination, as was Attwood. I knew what was happening behind the scenes. I knew what they were aiming at, and I didn't attend. Mzee never trusted Mboya because he knew Mboya was overly ambitious. He knew Mboya had the backing of the Americans to be in second place and be able to take over from the Mzee.

I'm sure it was put to Mzee that if Odinga is given too much of a free hand he might challenge the Old Man, and the threat of a communist takeover if Odinga was too powerful was probably impressed on the Old Man. But he should have realized that of all the people who were really honest with him, one was Odinga.

I didn't know I was being appointed to replace Odinga as Vice-President. I was never consulted. The President has the prerogative of changing his Ministers around at any time. I was at a Cabinet meeting when it was announced that I was the next Vice-President and I just looked surprised.

I was highly flattered, and to make matters even better, the President organized a little luncheon for me, in honour of the occasion, after the Cabinet meeting. He made a little speech about my work.

I would have liked to have stayed on as Foreign Minister, but nevertheless, if one is a Minister, one has to accept any movements. I think I was getting a bit too controversial in my handling of foreign policy, which was not to the liking of the Americans and the British. And I think certain pressures were put on the Old Man to get rid of me as Foreign Minister, and the Old Man thought of the brilliant idea of kicking me upstairs. This is what I just surmise, I have no clear proof.

But one indication is that when the Commonwealth Prime Ministers Conference was held in Lagos [in January 1966], at which time I was Foreign Minister, I was asked by the President to attend. But I was told that the delegation was to be led by James Gichuru. I said to the President,

'I'm afraid I won't go to Lagos. I never attend economic conferences, or lead the delegations to an economic conference, which I know nothing about, and Gichuru knows nothing about foreign affairs.' Well, I didn't attend. The day I was supposed to leave the Old Man rang me up in the morning and said, 'Joe, what time are you leaving this evening?' I said, 'I told you, I'm not going', and he stayed quiet, he didn't say anything. I said, 'I'm definitely not going to Lagos.'

Gichuru went and made a mess of it, because the question of Rhodesia was discussed there and he made a statement at Lagos saying that the Africans in Rhodesia were not fit for independence, or not ready for independence. He denied it of course when he came back. The Minister of Information at that time was Achieng Oneko and he actually got the videotape from Lagos to prove that Gichuru did make that statement. And when he was confronted with this fact in Parliament he denied it completely. Well, the tape was there to prove it.

My fears about Rhodesia were justified in the sense that I felt that Britain should have used force in bringing down the Smith regime. I always maintained that stand. Subsequent events have shown that Ian Smith, in spite of sanctions imposed upon Rhodesia by Britain, the United States and other countries, was still getting aid from South Africa.

The main issue is that Ian Smith was not prepared to come to terms with Robert Mugabe and Joshua Nkomo. And very much like the settlers in Kenya who wanted KADU to come into power so they would retain their influence, they found an equal partner like KADU in Bishop Muzorewa. Bishop Muzorewa is a stooge of the Europeans, and until you have a fair election in which the National Front can take part and you form a government which is one hundred percent African, you won't have any real peace in Rhodesia.

My mind was made up to leave Government when I was still Foreign Minister, after I got offered a job in the early part of '66 as chairman of Rothmans' new Kenya subsidiary, but it was not finalized until about May or June. Mzee announced my resignation at a Cabinet meeting as soon as he'd received my letter of resignation, but he did not want me to resign immediately. I said, 'It means, Mzee, I will lose my job.' He said, 'Well, Joe, you can still be the Chairman of Rothmans, but I want you to continue as Vice-President till the end of the year because I want you to attend the Commonwealth Prime Ministers Conference [in September] and I also want you to attend the OAU Heads of State Meeting and the Foreign Ministers Meeting. And then you can leave at the end of the year.' So I accepted that.

He did not appoint another Foreign Minister immediately. He kept that post for himself and it was months and months later that he appointed Njoroge Mungai as the Foreign Minister. Well, during that period the Old Man never really had an interest in foreign affairs. Things

## The President of the Republic of Kenya

The Hon. J. Murumbi, M.P.,
Vice-President of Kenya,
Office of the Vice-President,
Jogoo House,
NAIROBI

My dear Joe,

We have already discussed your letter of the 15th August intimating your wish to be relieved of your appointment as Vice-President, and agreed that this should take place at a convenient time towards the end of the year.

You have conveyed your wishes to me with the same straightforward honesty which has characterized our relationship throughout our long association and personal friendship. I greatly appreciate this.

During the struggle for Independence, and in the years of reconstruction since 1963, you have not spared yourself any effort which would advance the cause of our Party, our country and our people. When the time comes to write the history of these years, your personal contribution will be shown to have been among the greatest.

I have found you a wise and true Counsellor and a warm and loyal friend. Your departure from the Government will be a great loss, but I hope and trust that our long personal association and friendship will continue.

I wish you all success in the new field of endeavour to which you take your greatest talents. I wish to express to you my warm appreciation of all you have done and my continuing high regard for you as a person and as a patriot.

(signed Jomo Kenyatta)

PRESIDENT
September 23rd, 1966

began to go haywire. Various forces were at play, pulling our foreign policy in different directions. And then Mungai took over and of course he didn't really play his part as a Foreign Minister. I think in an interview he said that they were now more realistic about foreign affairs, and not so emotional. I think that was a kick at me.

I think Mungai was rather careless with foreign affairs. He wouldn't see Ambassadors, and the whole thing was left to slide. There was nobody at the helm controlling it, making foreign policy, and the result is that other elements in the Government with interests—favouring American interests, or British interests, or Israeli interests—all these forces came into play. Foreign affairs lost its sense of direction. I think the Government is now coming to realize there is still a lot to be done in our relations with the Arab countries, and it's not to say that improving relations with the Arab countries means to be anti-Israeli.

I wanted Mzee to confirm verbally to me that it was okay for me to leave at the end of the year, so on the 31st of December, 1966 I went to see him in Mombasa. I said, 'Mzee, I wanted to hear from you whether it is okay for me to leave. Today is my last day.' Charles Njonjo answered, 'Well, you're finished Joe, today is your last day.' But I think the Old Man didn't want me to leave. I think he was hurt, because he had been very good to me, and I don't think he wanted to say anything; he just turned his back on me.

There was no question of me making a dramatic exit. I didn't want to embarrass the Old Man in any way, I wanted to make it easier for him so that I could leave without rocking the boat.

## Why I Left Government

What influenced me mainly to leave Government was to see the change in people's minds that was taking place at that time. I realized that all the original good intentions we had of how to run the country, and how to look after the people who were poor or who had no land, had no jobs, these things were being forgotten. It was the personal interest of people which was paramount. I didn't want to be associated with a Government which was going to let down the people—not the educated people so much but the poor Kikuyus and members of other tribes who had taken part in the struggle, and who had faith in Kenyatta and all of us that we were going to give them a better deal. Freedom is not just saying you are free; freedom is bread and butter, improvement in the lives of the people. People looked up to us for hope. So that's why I felt I shouldn't stay in the system.

The question of my health was a minor problem, but I also realized that I would have been dead by now if I had stayed on. I was spending about six months, seven months, of the year out of the country, going from one country to the other. It's very hard stuff.

And the other factor which made it easier for me was that I was never involved in corruption. If you are, it's better to stay within the system because that's your protection. I was able to get out clean, and without any complications.

People enter politics because they have some ambitions to achieve something. I did not look at politics that way. Power never interested me. I felt that I was in the struggle for independence and when I was invited to become a Minister, I thought there was a contribution I could make, there was a job to be done, and everybody who was capable of doing a job should come forward to help. And that's what I've done.

I was not tribalistic in outlook. I've never looked at politics from a tribalistic angle, I've never looked at politics from a section or angle, I looked in a much broader perspective: that I have duty to do for my country.

I have never looked back and regretted the day I left politics. Never.

I feel I have a certain loyalty to Mzee; I wouldn't like to hurt him in any way by being too critical. We cannot ignore the fact that we have peace and stability in Kenya today because of him. But whether that peace and stability will survive after he's dead, I doubt very much.

His faults? I think promoting tribalism, promoting Kikuyu domination. That's something which may plunge the country into chaos, and if that really happens, people will blame him for that.

He could have been a great leader in the sense of maintaining the balance which he maintained in the beginning among the tribes. And we didn't have this Kikuyu domination in the beginning. But then he allowed himself to be influenced by certain elements amongst the Kikuyu and we have the situation which we have today, which could be dangerous. He has allowed himself to be influenced by other people, particularly members of the family—it's called the 'Royal Family'.

And, there are people who take advantage of him. I remember once in Mombasa, I was talking to him about corruption and Ministers and civil servants not being in their offices. 'Well, Joe,' he said, 'I know all about that. But you know, I'm in a difficult position; Ministers no longer tell me the truth.' There are people who have exploited him, people who take advantage of him, and more so now, in his old age. 'The Royal Family' take more advantage of him than he realizes but he can't do anything.

He could have stopped it before, some time ago, but not now. It's gone too far.

CHAPTER FOUR

# Art and the Search for Identity

### 'Decolonizing the Mind'

When people talk about Joseph Murumbi, they tend to discuss his roles as a political figure and as an art collector as though they were separate aspects of his life. But in fact, they were closely entwined. As a young clerk in Nairobi, he was becoming aware of the injustices of colonialism at the same time that he was trying his hand at sketching and painting. As an exile in London pleading Kenya's case to the world, he was also making regular forays to the antique shops in Portobello Road. And as Kenya's Foreign Minister travelling throughout Africa and beyond, he was regularly coming home laden with so many acquisitions that he needed help to get them all off the plane.

If anything, his passion for books was even greater, at least in his earlier years: he talks about foregoing lunch while he was in London in order to be able to afford a book he'd seen in a bookshop near his office.

Perhaps, as some suggest, Murumbi's interest in collecting can be seen as a manifestation of his search for identity. 'Murumbi was like a convert: converts are always the most passionate about proving their allegiance,' says Alan Donovan, Murumbi's African Heritage partner. 'When he "converted" to being Maasai he was extremely eager to prove the worth of being an African. Everything African was valuable to him. Whatever was African, he wanted to save it.

*Joseph Murumbi admires his collection of Ethiopian crosses and other art*

He knew how fast things were changing and disappearing. He would say, "We have to save this". He was very sensitive about who he was and how he got to be the person he was.' [65]

Dr Joyce Nyairo, a Kenyan academic and writer on cultural issues, shares this perception. 'He didn't ever fit into an Indian identity because he was not an Indian; he was seen as black in India,' Nyairo says. 'He wasn't Maasai either; he didn't know Maasai culture because he grew up in India.' Given these facts, she says, 'Culture became for him a way of exploring identity, of pursuing the unseen, the unacknowledged. What did it mean to be a Kenyan, an African, in the '50s and '60s?' [66]

Certainly the question Nyairo poses about what it meant to be African in the middle of the 20th Century was the same one that drove continent-wide efforts to throw off 'cultural imperialism'—a phrase which only came into wide use in the 1960s—along with political imperialism. Frantz Fanon, Leopold Senghor and others provided the intellectual and artistic underpinnings for the Negritude movement, for Pan-Africanism, and for celebrations of the pre-colonial past.

'There was an urgent need to uncover lost civilizations, republish texts, and write the forgotten histories of Africa's people,' writes cultural historian Derek R Peterson in his introduction to *The Politics of Heritage in Africa*. Describing the perceived role of artists, musicians and writers as being to recover 'a sovereign way of life' and, in Ngugi wa Thiongo's words, to 'decolonize the mind', [67] he describes the mid-20th Century heritage search as 'a salvage operation'; heritage 'was something that had to be "discovered" or "reclaimed".' [68]

Collecting can be seen as part of that process. In West Africa, says Johanna Zetterstrom-Sharp, a British Academy post-doctoral fellow, collecting was in fact not a new undertaking but went back hundreds of years. One example she cites is the 'Benin bronzes', a collection of thirteenth century artworks in the palace at Benin City. Individual chiefs, she says, typically kept collections of objects used on ceremonial occasions. [69]

The importance with which collecting is viewed in West Africa is reflected in a comment in 2016 by Prince Yemisi Shyllon of Nigeria, reputed to own the largest art collection in Africa. 'I don't believe collections should just be about collecting and enjoying art. I think it should go beyond just collecting—it should go into the element of propagating the culture or the heritage of the people and way of life of the people,' he told a CNN interviewer. [70]

*Joseph Murumbi with one of the prized items in his collection – an ivory-handled knife*

*Art and the Search for Identity*

## A Lone Voice

Africans in the eastern part of the continent have been much slower than their West African counterparts to embrace collecting. Murumbi was unique or nearly so in the early independence era and remains unusual even today among Eastern Africans with regard to his interest in collecting and preserving books, art and artefacts of all kinds. His interest in books gave him a bond with at least two West African leaders, Kwame Nkrumah, the first president of Ghana, and Dr Nnamdi Azikiwe, the first president of Nigeria.

The lack of interest in collecting among eastern Africans may have been partly due to the relative paucity of sophisticated cultural objects such as existed in West African countries. It was also probably due to the widespread influence of Christian missionaries, who had caused many Africans in eastern Africa to abandon their traditional practices and dress and to feel embarrassed about anything that suggested they were other than 'modern'.

'In Murumbi's time art was still on the periphery,' notes Nyairo. 'The British wiped out traditional culture and made people feel their culture was inferior. In Murumbi's time the aesthetic was Western.' [71] Similarly, Zarina Patel, managing editor of *AwaaZ* magazine in Nairobi, says of Murumbi: 'His very presence influenced culture and awareness of culture. Until him, there was no public figure involved in anything like that.' [72]

What Murumbi did through his support of African Heritage was to help make traditional art legitimate, Nyairo says. 'I think African Heritage spoke to ordinary Kenyans mainly through fashion and music,' she says. 'The rest may have been chic among the elite but not ordinary people. But what they did at African Heritage was to make people feel they could do art. Someone making beads hadn't thought there was a market for them; they were just a personal thing. But African Heritage created an awareness of the market. You could argue that the Maasai Market—a gathering of sellers of African products held in different locations around Nairobi—'is in a direct line from that. And young people go to Maasai Market.' [73]

Not everything Murumbi collected was of equal value but, as Donovan puts it, all of it was a

*Joseph and Sheila Murumbi in the library at their Muthaiga home*

reflection of his personal tastes. Donovan disdains the notion, still widespread among museums, that any item that hasn't been used in a ceremony or everyday life isn't 'authentic'.

'Most of the masks and sculptures in Africa, especially those of wood, were either eaten by woodworm or burned by the colonialists and missionaries, and shunned by those who would normally use them for ceremonial purposes as being devil worship,' says Donovan. 'Most of the items at African Heritage could be considered "copies" in that they were not used in ceremonies because this market dried up. So generations of craftsmen and carvers turned to tourists and outsiders. But if you are talking about the ethnographic items like weapons, containers, artefacts, textiles and other items, then these are all genuine used items, many over 50 years old and most of which are vanishing and disappearing like the ceremonial objects before them.'[74]

According to Zetterstrom-Sharp, the making of objects for sale rather than use goes back to

*Joseph Murumbi in his Muthaiga home library*

the earliest days of European involvement in Africa and was widespread on the continent. Such objects were often made with just as much skill as earlier versions, she argues, mentioning as an example a Sierra Leonean carver who believes he is inhabited by the same spirit when he's making masks for sale as when he's making them for ceremonies. [76]

Murumbi was remarkable not just for pursuing his collecting in the face of relative indifference among his African peers but also for his awareness of the importance of objects in reconstructing the past. Just how valuable even seemingly mundane items can be in this effort was reflected in a letter published in the *Daily Nation* in 2003, urging that nothing that Murumbi had collected be allowed to leave the country. The writer, Ignatius Mwenda Ngore of Meru, described his own failure to complete a sociological history of pre-colonial Meru because 'it proved impossible to trace a single shield, sword or club used by their warriors'. [76]

Murumbi was also important for championing contemporary artists. Elkana Ongesa, the first Kenyan artist to exhibit at African Heritage, was one such artist. It was thanks to the fact that Murumbi had one of Ongesa's works at his house, where it was seen by the director of UNESCO, that Ongesa was commissioned to create a large sculpture in front of the UNESCO headquarters in Paris. [77]

## The Role of Museums

In the late 1970s, at the time when Murumbi was trying to decide what to do with his personal collection of books and art, museums in Kenya and elsewhere were already a well-established phenomenon. But according to Kenyan Professor Karega-Munene (his full name), the management of the National Museum of Kenya was still for the most part whites-only, and its focus was primarily on pre-history and fossils—owing no doubt at least in part to the influence

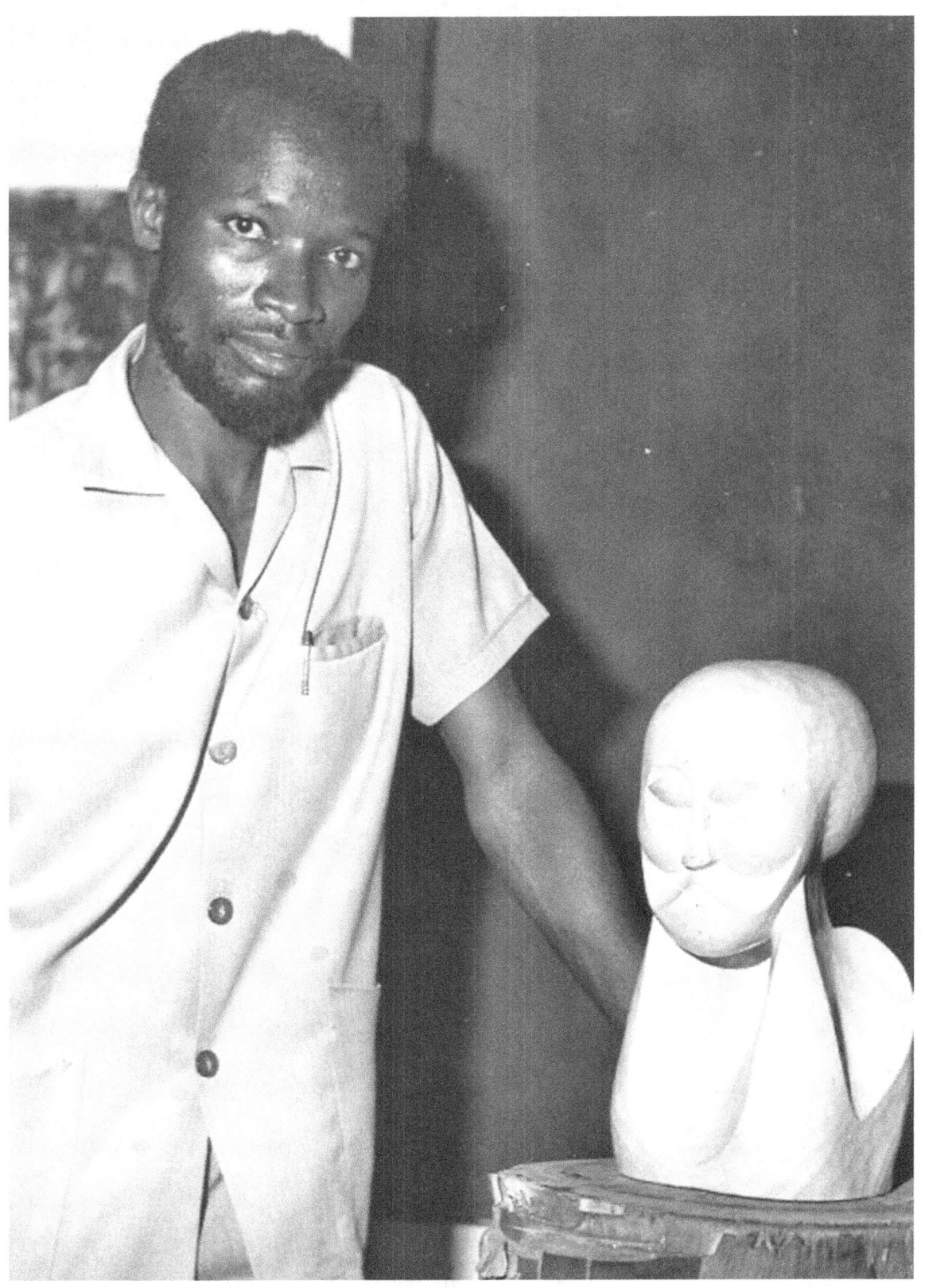
*Elkana Ongesa, one of the artists Murumbi championed*

of an early curator, palaeontologist Louis Leakey.[78] Indeed, according to Karega-Munene, a plan prepared in the mid-'60s called for having 'scientific museums' which would be national, and 'cultural museums' housed in constructions built of traditional materials and overseen by non-professional staff.[79]

It wasn't until the late 1990s that there was more official emphasis on culture, according to Karega-Munene, and only in 2006 was an Act passed that charged the National Museum with being responsible for identifying and transmitting 'culture and national heritage' to the public.[80] Even now, however, most Kenyans aren't regular museum-goers, and, according to Nyairo, they don't view museums as essential to the life of the country. 'Preserving art is still seen as a luxury,' she says.[81]

**IN MURUMBI'S WORDS**

# Art and the Search for Identity

My father read a lot, but I don't think he was a collector of books. After I read the two books he gave me about Kenya and India, I began to read other books and try to find other books. There happened to be a bookshop opposite the present Ambassador Hotel in Nairobi, and I used to spend a lot of time there on Saturdays and Sundays. I picked up a lot of books on Africa and on Kenya and that made me interested in building up a library about Kenya. And I think I built up a library of about 600 books. I left those with a friend of mine when I went to Somalia and they all disappeared.

When I came back I started collecting again; before I went to India I had about 300 books. And when I went to England I started collecting more books. I used to go over to Kegan Paul, a book dealer opposite the British Museum. I started first of all collecting books on Kenya. What happens is that as you buy books, you come to know of other books, and you look for them, and also books on Africa in general. Eventually I had two or three thousand books.

One day Sheila was talking to a book dealer in London about books, and this book dealer was looking for a book called *Through Maasailand* by Joseph Thompson. Sheila said, 'If I can get you the second edition, how much will you offer me?' He said, 'I'll give you £2.10'. She knew that I had two copies of the second edition so she came home and said, 'Look here, would you like to sell a copy of *Through Maasailand*?' So I looked at my copies, and the copy without a map I had paid three shillings for, and the perfect copy with the map I had paid two shillings for, and the thought struck me that there was some money in this business.

We put out a book catalogue which mainly was of books about South Africa which I didn't want, and I sent it out to about twenty people. I didn't get very much response. Later I decided: let's do this systematically. We went to the Westminster Library and we got the addresses of most of the important libraries through the world—about a hundred and fifty universities. I made a more comprehensive catalogue of books on Africa in general, and we sent this out, and we got a very good response.

We used to spend our weekends combing the south of England for books, and we were able to put out a catalogue every two months. And we found we were making some money on it and this helped me a great deal to buy more books for my own library.

We had a little flat which was just one room, a bedsitter; it was a small room which had a bath and a kitchen. I used to park all my newspapers in the bath. On top of the bath was a cover, and it was loaded with books. So whenever we wanted a bath, we had to take the books off the cover and take all the newspapers out, and then have a bath.

I sold one very valuable book which was called *Leo Africanus* published in 1600, the first English edition. Sheila had found it in a bookshop in South Kensington, and the price at that time was £52, which was an enormous sum for me. But when I had some money I rang up the owner and I said, 'Have you still got that book, *Leo Africanus*?' He said, 'Yes, I've still got it'. So I went down to his shop and I went in and I said, 'I've come to collect that book'. And I said, 'Have you got anything else?' So he pulled out some other books. And, just as he did that, a man came in and said, 'I want to buy that *Leo Africanus*'. The owner said, 'I'm very, very sorry, I've just sold it to this gentleman'. And we decided to put it in my catalogue at £98. The book today is worth about £2,500.

On another occasion later, I bought a small book which was in loose-leaf manuscript form. There was a little bit of paper in it saying, 'Part of the loot from the Palace of Abubakar, Sultan of Nupe, captured during the Bida Campaign' [a colonial war in 1897]. And I also bought another one which had a little typewritten note said 'Extracts of the Koran in the Kanuri language of Northern Nigeria'. There was a leather binder and a bit of leather which you wrapped around and tied it with a string. And I paid five pounds for one and three pounds for the other. I brought them back to Kenya. When I was going to Ghana and to Nigeria I thought I would see Dr Azikiwe in Nigeria and offer him these two books. Well, I stopped off at Accra

*A cover illustration from one of Murumbi's African art books*

and I was with Nkrumah in his office and we were discussing books, so I told him about these two books. He said he'd buy them. In order to put him off, I said £500. And he said, 'It's a deal'.

When I came back to Kenya, my books arrived about two months later, by sea. I went down to Mombasa and every one of the cases was opened, and there was a horde of customs officials going through each box, and a number of my books were confiscated. Later we learned the police had burned them.

## Artist to Art Collector

My interest in collecting art developed at a later stage. I always was interested in art, and used to do a bit of drawing myself while working as a clerk in the Medical Department [in the 1930s]. Doctor Hale used to encourage me to draw and paint more. One day he suggested, 'Why don't you exhibit your pictures in the Arts & Crafts Society?' I didn't take any notice of it for about two years and then the year I decided to exhibit, the Arts & Crafts Society decided that they would not accept any paintings or any art from Africans or Asians. I went along to the secretary, who turned out to be Mervyn Hill, who was also the secretary of the Agricultural Society and later on became the editor of the *Kenya Weekly News*. I said, 'What's the meaning of this ban on Africans and Asians?' He said, 'Well, we get art from Africans and Asians but we don't understand it.' I said, 'Is it you personally who don't understand or your committee?' He said, 'We all don't understand it.'

I said, 'I'm going to say this very bluntly to you: I don't think any of you understand what art means.'

He said, 'Why don't you bring your pictures here and we'll have a look at them and see whether we can accept them.' I think there were six pictures, some of them paintings and some of them black and white. They were all accepted for exhibition. But I could not exhibit them directly in the exhibition, I had to exhibit them through a member of the Arts & Crafts Society and my pictures were put in a loan section. And one picture in particular was highly commended and I was asked to appear there and to meet the Governor who congratulated me on the best picture in the loan section. It was a charcoal and chalk drawing of a child's head, done from pure imagination.

What I'm trying to illustrate here is that the prejudice that everything African was taboo and that we have to accept everything European was wrong. Because African art is highly prized and highly appreciated today in Europe and America. People like Picasso and to a certain extent Henry Moore were collectors of African art and it influenced their work to a great extent. Very good, old, African art today fetches a very high price; in other words, it is appreciated just like people pay fabulous prices for European art and Chinese art.

My collecting started toward the end of my stay in England. I happened to go to a junk shop near Camden Town where I found a small carved tusk which I liked very much, and the man sold it to me for about £2.10. Well, today I think it's worth at least over a hundred pounds. He told me, 'I'd rather sell it to you because you're from Africa and it should go back to Africa.' And from that one piece I began.

We used to go to Portobello Market in London, not that I had any money, but even looking at things gave me a lot of pleasure. And then when I had some money from dealing in books, I used to spend a little bit of this on buying pieces of African art.

Later, when I was a Minister of the Government, I used to travel considerably in Africa, and wherever I went I normally saved my allowance, because we enjoyed the hospitality of the governments wherever we went, and I used that money to buy art.

Then later on, when I left Government and was in business, I had more money and I was able to spend on things which I found or when I went abroad. And then finally, of course, we opened African Heritage. And that gave me the opportunity to get some good pieces, because I had first choice when these things came to the shop.

## *The Joy of Collecting*

African art is a very broad field. One aspect is traditional African art. Then there is modern art, which includes works like those of the Makonde, which are very stylized abstract. And thirdly is the commercialized African art.

To understand African art and to appreciate African art and to collect African art one has to go much deeper than just looking at it, and understand the significance of it. I have some large tusks that have been carved very crudely, with very crude figures, probably done before the Portuguese went to Angola. Now, following on that, when the Portuguese took over their colonies of West Africa, certain pieces were made to order, showing Portuguese figures, people with hats, jackets with buttons on them, an umbrella.

A small wooden statue studded with nails and little bits of metal comes from what is today the Democratic Republic of the Congo. A lot of these statues have been produced in that part of the world and they are fetishes. If you look at the form of it, it has little bits of glass in the eyes, and another bit of glass on the stomach. Now, either the head was hollowed out or the stomach was hollowed out and into this certain charms were inserted. In various ways hunters were protected when they went out, or people's love affairs were enhanced. These fetishes are rather rare pieces.

The little ivory head in my collection was used by a society called Bwami Association in the Eastern Congo. These little carvings are generally handed down within the family and they represent the link between the living and the dead.

Why there are not more Africans interested in art, I don't know. But I think it will come in the course of time. It's rather an expensive hobby today if you want to start collecting really genuine pieces, which are extremely rare and very highly priced. I think Africans must start collecting contemporary works of art which are being produced by some very fine artists. If our people begin to collect these pieces, then I think they will begin to spend more money and more time

*Murumbi studies a carved ivory tusk from the Congo, the first piece of African art he ever bought*

collecting older pieces of African art.

My interest in stamps began while I was in school in India. There was a fellow called Edwin Athaide who used to collect stamps, and he started me off. But I don't know what happened to my schoolboy collection—I probably lost it or gave it away to somebody. Then I inherited a collection from my father which was a nice collection of East African stamps, which I sold one day when I was in need of money, for about three hundred shillings. And about five or six years ago I started collecting again, and I have now got a very good collection of East African stamps.

I prefer to spend my money on art, stamps, and things which give one pleasure. And besides that, it's an investment which is appreciating much faster than money in a bank. I've never had money stashed away in a bank. If I have any money I spend it on buying art or books or stamps.

## The Importance of Culture

Culture is the life of a people, the habits of the people, the art of a people, the folklore of people. We were under colonial rule for many years. And during that time all our African values were denounced and we were told to accept whatever the European had to offer us.

We now live in the modern world and therefore we need to use the cultures, knowledge, and education of the Western world in order to keep up with the Western world, but we must not lose the sense that we are Africans; that we have our own identity, our own values, and some of those are very good.

For instance, in the Western world you electrocute a man or hang him for an offence. In Africa if somebody committed a murder and he was tried through tribal custom—I'm talking about the past—he was brought before the tribal elders and if it was found that he had really committed the murder, then he had to pay compensation to the family of the deceased. Well, I

*Tuareg warriors, as shown in an illustration in one of Murumbi's books on African art*

think that was a more humane attitude than just putting a man in an electric chair or hanging him.

Some Europeans may say that our art is very crude, but if you look around the world today you'll see the influence of African art on some famous artists like Picasso and Chagall. Some of the national dishes of Brazil are African. The black man in America has influenced music, acting—modern jazz springs from West African music.

You'll find that although the West Africans are educated, they still believe in their local traditions: the dancing, the folklore, the art. The Japanese are a highly industrialised country today but they still maintain in their homes their own Japanese tradition and custom. That is what I'm saying is important: not to lose our African background, our African culture and the cultural values behind it.

I don't say that in any sense to condemn European or other art—in my collection I have art from all over the world—but I'm talking about African culture and cultural values which we must not lose sight of. There is a contribution which we can make, as Africans, to the common pool of the world's culture. But in the first place we must be proud of ourselves.

CHAPTER FIVE

# The Later Years

## Into the Private Sector

Murumbi's departure from Government at the end of 1966 passed without much comment. There were other, bigger political stories at the time, most particularly what was happening to Oginga Odinga and his new party, KPU. The Kenyatta Government had already reinstated detention without trial in mid-1966, and several KPU leaders were soon thereafter arrested and detained.

Over the next few years, Kenya experienced a period of intense and sometimes violent political struggles. Bildad Kaggia, once Kenyatta's fellow prisoner in Kapenguria, was mocked by Kenyatta for his lack of personal wealth, while Kenyatta and his family grew rich on land and 'presents' from those seeking favours. Kenyatta himself, once the all-powerful leader, suffered a heart attack in 1968 and was in declining health thereafter, leaving intrigues to swirl through the halls of Parliament and beyond.

When Kenyatta came to power 'he was already an old man,' notes Professor Muriuki. 'He became sickly early on in his presidency. And that led to a situation where those around him—the Kiambu mafia—began to scheme to see who would take over from him, people like Njoroge Mungai, people like James Gichuru. Toward the end of his presidency Kenyatta was not in control. It was the Kiambu mafia who were really in control.' [82]

*The Later Years*

Murumbi remained a nominal Member of Parliament until the end of the session in 1969, but stayed completely out of active politics for the rest of his life. His first job in the private sector was as chairman of a Kenya subsidiary set up in 1966 by the cigarette company Rothmans, but this post did not last long. Rothmans concluded by November of 1967 that it could not successfully compete with British American Tobacco and sold its assets to BAT at a substantial loss. Subsequently, Murumbi became a well-paid director of a number of other corporations, and also a co-founder of African Heritage, whose Nairobi gallery became a must-see for visitors.

According to Alan Donovan, Murumbi's partner in African Heritage, the idea for the gallery grew out of his meeting Murumbi in 1970 at a display of artefacts Donovan had collected in Turkana. 'Meeting him changed my life,' says Donovan. 'At the time I had run out of money and I was planning to go back to the US Murumbi said, "Would you go back to Turkana and make a collection for me?" I responded yes without hesitation. He was the first and only African collector I ever knew.' [83]

Donovan says, 'It was his dream to have a Pan-African centre in Nairobi where artists from all

*Murumbi in front of one of his magnificent Lamu doors and clay pots from Portugal that came down to Kenya duing the dhow trade. The doors were taken away by unknown persons after the house was allowed to deteriorate. The pots are displayed at the Nairobi Gallery.*

over the world could come and have their works shown. And I was sort of the one to implement his dream.' [84] According to Donovan, 'By the time I met him he had more or less finished with collecting; he relied on me to do the collecting. But he had contacts himself with artists.' [85]

When African Heritage began in 1973, Murumbi brought in a third partner, an Italian, but according to Donovan the man didn't last long. 'The guy cheated in a fishing competition and when Joe heard that, that was the end,' Donovan recalls. [86] Later, they took on another partner, but after Murumbi's death Donovan became the sole owner. [87]

In his book *My Journey Through African Heritage*, Donovan describes how African Heritage grew from a gallery in downtown Nairobi to a multi-faceted enterprise that included international fashion shows and workshops producing carvings and jewellery for export. In one interview reproduced in the book, he reports that at its peak in the early 1990s, African Heritage had over 500 employees on its payroll and 51 outlets worldwide. Ten years later, however, the company collapsed owing to factors including a severe decline in tourism to Kenya and increased competition from other African countries. [88]

As Donovan explains it, Murumbi 'was not involved in African Heritage day-to-day. But he was helpful in getting money for travel and dealing with things like travel problems because he still had contacts in Government. So without him it would have been very difficult.' [89]

*Alan Donovan shows the Mayor of Nairobi, Margaret Kenyatta, a Turkana wooden dipper while Joe Murumbi looks on at the opening of the first gallery of African Heritage on Kenyatta Avenue where the I&M Tower is today.*

*The Later Years*

*Fire razes the African Heritage Gallery in 1976*

## Looking to the Future

In the late 1970s, Murumbi decided it was time to dispose of his papers and most of his library and art collection. He held discussions with several institutions and in the end struck a deal with the Kenya National Archives, which he himself had been instrumental in setting up while he was Vice-President. Included in Murumbi's vision was a plan for the Government to turn his house in Muthaiga, which he'd bought after leaving government, into a centre for African studies, with his library and art collection kept intact. He called this 'a dream very close to my heart'.

Professor Godfrey Muriuki was a member of the Kenya National Archives advisory committee that negotiated with Murumbi for much of his collection of books, art and papers. 'When we were discussing the sale he said, "If I sold this overseas I would make more money,"' Muriuki recalls. 'But —and this is where I say he was very patriotic—he said, "No, I don't want to sell it to America or Britain because it belongs to Kenya and I would like it to remain in Kenya, so long as you give me a little bit of money to cover the costs of collecting this material".'[90]

Murumbi sold his Muthaiga house and plot to the Government in late 1977 for Ksh 2.2 million, on the understanding that a research centre would be established there. He also sold his library and much of his art collection to the Government for Ksh 4 million. (The total would be equal to about Ksh 468 million, or about £3.4 million, in 2018 terms.)

Murumbi 'pioneered the idea of archiving in Kenya' says Zahid Rajan, executive editor of *AwaaZ* magazine in Nairobi. 'No one thought about it in the 1960s. Now we take it for granted.'[91] But perhaps not as much as might ideally be the case, Nyairo says. 'We have a history of neglect,' she says. 'We celebrate oral history so much that we don't think about the written word.'[92]

As Murumbi was well aware, just as with cultural artefacts, much of Kenya's documentary heritage had been removed by the British. And British officials, recognizing its potentially explosive nature, were not about to let such records come back. As early as 1967 the Kenya government asked the British government for discussions on the topic, but that request along with similar requests later were either ignored or rebuffed.

The Mau Mau period records were clearly the ones of most concern. In May, 1961, the Secretary of State for the Colonies sent guidance to colonial officials in Kenya and elsewhere telling them that before any records could be turned over to independent governments a committee consisting of a special branch officer and two senior administrative officers must go through them to ensure that nothing would be turned over that might embarrass the Government or any member of the police, military forces or public servants. Subsequently 1,500 files in 307 boxes were sent from Kenya to the UK, the vast majority of which related to the State of Emergency, including information about detainees and detention camps.[93]

According to Anne Thurston, who after her time in Kenya went on to become an expert in international records management, in the 1970s she and Kenyan colleagues were told by the British Foreign and Commonwealth Office that the Kenyan records held by the British Government would never be made available. However, the Mau Mau records surfaced during a court case decided in 2012 in which several surviving Mau Mau detainees successfully sought the right to claim damages for the abuses they had suffered, and Kenya continues to seek the records' return.

## Return to the Land

At the same time that he was considering what to do with his collections, Murumbi was also deciding to move to Maasailand. In 1977, thanks to his Maasai heritage, he obtained about 2,000 acres for a farm and ranch in Trans Mara, in an area known as Intona, and built a 35-room mansion that was to be his and Sheila's retirement home. His intention was to raise high-quality cattle and inspire the Maasai to do the same.

Donovan recalls with amusement the arrival of the Murumbis at their new property as in keeping with their Nairobi style. Donovan himself was already there, waiting for them, at the home of a local priest with whom the Murumbis had arranged to initially stay. 'The priest had a little house and had given up his bedroom for them,' Donovan says. 'They finally arrived pulling a trailer. We watched these cases of alcohol—whiskey, bourbon, champagne—and foodstuffs get unloaded. The food kept coming and piling up around us, where we were sitting. The priest said, "Joe, you know we have a simple life here." And Joe said, "That's what I want."' [94]

For all of Murumbi's appreciation of the finer things in life, however, Donovan says he was never 'grand'. 'I think he strove to cultivate a reputation of being urbane,' Donovan says, 'I think that was part of his persona.' [95] But, he says, 'Even though he loved rich, opulent things, including his home, a place showing that he had money and taste, he was still a person whom a common man would feel was on their side, which I always marvelled at.'

Donovan remembers Murumbi as having had a largely European circle of friends owing to similar tastes. But Pheroze Nowrojee, a leading Nairobi lawyer who was close to Sheila Murumbi after Joseph Murumbi's death, says that the friends of theirs that he met through Sheila were a widely diverse group, including Asians, Arabs and Africans as well as Europeans. Included in this group, he says, was Bildad Kaggia, whom he remembers visiting with Sheila long after Kaggia's political days were over. [96]

**IN MURUMBI'S WORDS**

# The Later Years

Very few people know that when Rothmans wanted to open up a factory in Nairobi, I insisted that they should make part of the equity available to local people. They wanted to start a fully-owned Rothmans in this country but I said, 'That won't work. We've got to keep some of the profits in the country, because if you give part of the equity to the local people, and part of the profits remain here, people will have more confidence in the company and your security lies in local participation.'

Some of the Ministers wanted shares themselves, free shares. But I said, no, you're not going to get them.

We were competitors of British American Tobacco. I think BAT used some influence to persuade the Old Man and others to make it difficult for us. Eventually we decided the best thing to do was to pull out. So we sold our assets to BAT. One good thing was that we paid every shareholder—African, European or whoever—at the par value [the amount the purchaser originally paid] of their shares. We were the first company in Kenya that opened shares to the general public. And after that other companies have done the same.

I obtained several directorships, for instance Bamburi Cement, Portland Cement, Kenya Construction Company and African Heritage.

The idea of African Heritage was to open a shop selling African art, good African art and crafts, in the hope that the people of Kenya would begin to realize the beauty of African art and also collect it as an investment. We set up shop on Nairobi's main Kenyatta Avenue and we did quite well. However, most of our business was confined to tourists coming to Kenya and the volume of business with local people was negligible.

We tried to encourage African artists as much as possible: we held exhibitions for them, bought items from them, and we imported a considerable amount of goods from many parts of Africa.

When I left Government and was in business, I had more money that I was able to spend on things which I found or when I went abroad. And when we opened African Heritage, that gave me an opportunity to get some good pieces, because I had first choice whenever Alan Donovan returned from his buying trips to other African countries or when items would come into the gallery.

Our house in Muthaiga was built about fifty years ago by a man named Klein. He was an American big game hunter from California, and the style of the house was old Californian architecture, Spanish-Moorish architecture. I had seen this house during the war when I used

*Joseph Murumbi at an 'African Heritage Night', in the company of JM Kariuki, left, and Prince Patrick of Toro*

to come up to Muthaiga to the Army Headquarters when I was being recruited to serve in Somalia, and I used to stand outside the gates and admire the house. The garden is a most pleasant garden with indigenous trees that I am very fond of. We spent a lot of time and energy on it.

We began collecting European art in the last five or six years, and we've been able to blend African art and European art in the house, which has been appreciated by many people. Many people think that you cannot blend the two along with Indian art. But there's art from all over the world in the house and it blends quite well.

## Responding to Racism

Muthaiga used to be a very exclusive area, and most of the Ambassadors lived here, business executives lived here, and the title deeds expressly said that land or houses could not be bought here by non-Europeans, and non-Europeans could stay here only if they were servants. The same thing applied to the Muthaiga Club. I became a member after leaving Government because the Duke of Manchester, who is a friend of mine, asked me to join the club. I said, 'Manny, I will only become a member if I'm not subjected to being interviewed by three members of the committee', who were supposed to come to your house and see how you lived and what kind of person you were and so on. I said, 'I will only join the club if they accept me as I am. I am not going to be subjected to an interview.' And later all he said was that I'd been accepted.

The Muthaiga Country Club is the last stronghold of the European settler type; you can see

*Joe and Sheila Murumbi at their Muthaiga home with a statue by Francis Nnaggenda*

*The Later Years*

when a black man walks in—there are now both African and Asian members of the club—they look at you as if to say, 'This is not the place for you, it is only for white people.'

Sometimes I've had the experience of very silly Europeans shouting at me or something, but I never stay quiet, I go up to that person and say, 'Look here, you must understand that this country is not yours anymore. You may be a citizen, or you may be a non-citizen, I don't know what your status is, but you have to respect us and if you respect me, I'll respect you. But if you try to misbehave, you may find yourself out of the country.'

I think that the reasons why some of these people remained was that they had large vested interests in Kenya, either in farms or businesses, and they were of an age where it was impossible for them to start a new life elsewhere. And it's convenient to stay here. I used to use an extract from a *Kenya Weekly News*, which I one day found, about Mrs So-and-So who was enjoying her holiday in the UK, and had come to the conclusion that Kenya is a much better place to live because if you are in England you've got to do your own washing up, you've got to do your own cooking, you've got to do your own shopping, and even Major-Generals wash up.

Many Europeans left the country, either through being afraid of reactions from Africans, or through not being prepared to stay in Kenya because they couldn't live in a country ruled by Africans. If Kenya had become a white-dominated country I'm quite sure the policies of the white man would have drifted towards those of South Africa and Rhodesia.

*Joseph Murumbi with Chief Archivist Dr Maina Kagombe*

## Parting with the Past

I had an Africana Library of about 6,000 or 7,000 volumes. I had a very sizeable African art collection and apart from that is the European art, African art, and a collection of postage stamps and also my personal papers. I felt the time had come when the library, my personal papers, and some of the African art should go to the Government and it should be preserved in a library—a Government library. But I'm not a Rockefeller or a Morgan, millionaires who can afford to donate these things to the nation. I've got to live, and in case I die, I've got my wife to provide for, and who's going to look after her or me if I give everything away to the Government for nothing?

So I approached the University in Nairobi and told them that this library's for sale and would they like to buy it. They said they were interested but they didn't pursue the matter any further. And then I approached the museums, Richard Leakey in the National Museum, and they were interested; and then the Archives came to know about it and they were also interested. And then another body, the Academy of Sciences, was keenly interested and said they could raise the money. But nobody came forward with the money.

I went to [then Finance Minister Mwai] Kibaki and said, 'Kibaki, there are so many people interested in my library. I want to sell it, I wanted the Government to buy it, but nobody talks about the money. Has the Government got the money?' He told me that about two years before the University had approached the Government for funds to buy the library and the funds were still there. So I told him, 'If the money's there, why don't we negotiate?'

The people who were very keen at that moment were the Archives. So the negotiations started with the Archives and they finally agreed upon a price for the African art, the library and for my personal papers. And then they said they had no place to display the items so they were interested in the house as well.

When these talks were going on about the disposal of my library, the Chief Archivist, Dr

Maina Kagombe, used the powers in the legislation drawn up by me when the Archives were started during the time I was Vice-President. There were no Archives before that. According to the legislation, the Chief Archivist has the powers to ban the export of any documents which are of public interest to the Kenya Government. So a ban was placed on the export of my books.

It was rumoured that I was going to sell my library abroad. Well, I've had a lot of enquiries from abroad and particularly from universities in the United States, but I have never had any intention of selling it abroad. In my will, which was made about 15 years ago, I bequeathed the library on my death to my wife. There was a stipulation that she could sell the library, but the library should not leave Kenya. So there was that safeguard.

That library was built up on a great sacrifice. Sometimes when I was in London I spent my lunch money on buying a book. I'd be on Charing Cross Road where all these book shops are and I'd find a book which I wanted and I gave up my lunch and bought the book. And I'd hate to see this whole thing disappear.

The Archives should have been started immediately we were independent. We had already lost important documents, for instance from the Mau Mau period. Just before independence the British Government—the Kenya Government of that time—either destroyed or sent away all the files relative to this period. So we have very little material available in Kenya for our Archives. Now it's time that we begin to build up our documentation. It's a very expensive process, but the Government should try to accumulate in one spot as much as is possible of the documentation that is of historical interest and that would be of use to researchers.

## *Intona*

When I was thinking of going back to Maasailand a friend of mine told me: 'Why don't you go above the escarpment between Lolgorian and Kilgoris, you will find some beautiful land there.' So Sheila and I left Nairobi and we spent the night at Kericho. It was a Saturday morning and we left Kericho and we motored right down from Kilgoris to Lolgorian on to the Migori River. I was fascinated with the land, which was so beautiful—it was virgin land, unspoilt, with forests and rivers and open glades—that I fell in love with it immediately. And so did Sheila.

The next day the committee of the Olalui Group Ranch was meeting, and they invited me. Some of the members of the committee were elderly people who knew me when I was young and knew my mother, and my mother's people, the Uasin Gishu Maasai. My cousin who was the Member of Parliament for the area, Mr John Konchella, introduced me.

We eventually got our land and this area is called Intona. It's rather peculiar because Intona is a Maasai word and it means 'roots' which is really the case; I have gone back to settle among my mother's people. I feel very grateful to the chairman of the committee who so spontaneously and willingly helped me to get this land. They wanted me to come and settle down here and they told me, 'We want you to help us to develop.'

The Maasai are cattlemen, they are pastoralists, and I want to keep good cattle here so the Maasai can see how they can benefit from keeping better stock. To the Maasai it doesn't matter whether it's a small animal or a big animal, it's the number that counts. But I think if you confront a Maasai with two animals, one a well-bred animal, a fat animal, a big animal, and compare that animal with a Maasai animal which is very poor, standing hardly three feet off the ground, I think he will see the difference between the two animals and gradually you can get them to change their position to where they assess the quality of their cattle as wealth.

You can also grow other crops—maize, coffee, tea, barley, wheat, oats—but it is essentially cattle country and it can produce enough beef for Kenya, it can produce enough beef for export. And apart from that I think I'm going to go for bee-keeping in a very big way. There are also possibilities of fish farming and there may be a market for fish in the surrounding towns of Kisii, Kericho, Sotik, and even as far as Nakuru. And if I have a deep freeze I could freeze the fish and then sell it.

Sheila looks after me and takes part in the management of the farm and now that we are building a new home she is very busy trying to find things for it. She is a source of solace, somebody who shares my worries, shares my interests, and is a full partner on the farm. She has got a heart of gold and is very kind to people. That's what makes her so lovable and my workers all respect her.

I've come to this farm, to this land, having left the town life of Nairobi. At a certain stage in one's life, one wants peace and quiet, and this peace and quiet I can find here. I'm very glad that Sheila is just as keen as I am. She's now come to hate Nairobi and I hate Nairobi, and we just go to Nairobi when we feel we have to go for some business or other reason, but otherwise we prefer to stay here on the land. There are lots of challenges, lots of opportunities to build something up from scratch.

*The Murumbis at their new home, Intona, in Maasailand*

*Joseph Murumbi, in traditional Maasai attire including a lion mane, at his Intona home*

*Postscript*

# JOSEPH MURUMBI
## A LEGACY OF INTEGRITY

POSTSCRIPT

By Alan Donovan's account, the Murumbis were very happy at Intona. But within a few years Murumbi's failing health—he suffered a stroke and later a fall at Intona in 1982 that left him in almost constant pain—forced the couple to return to Nairobi. In the years that followed, the Intona property, on which Murumbi had a substantial loan, became the source of endless fights between local residents, descendants on his mother's side, and the lending institution. The house itself is now a ruin.

Meanwhile, back in Nairobi, the Murumbis' Muthaiga house, after being sold to the Government, was first renovated and then, several years later, demolished. Murumbi's library and art were taken to the Kenya National Archives building, where for years they were mostly left in boxes in the basement.

The Muthaiga property was then subdivided and sold for the suspiciously low total price of Ksh 234,000 to well-connected individuals including a son of then-President Moi. 'Halfway through the demolition', according to an article in the *Daily Nation*, 'an unbelieving, ailing Murumbi went to see for himself what he was hearing. As he went around the plot in a wheel-chair, he could hardly believe what he was witnessing.' [97]

In Donovan's opinion, it was the shock of seeing what had happened that killed Murumbi.

*Joseph Murumbi, shortly before he died in 1990 in Nairobi*

*Postscript*

He died on 21 June, 1990.

Murumbi, along with his wife who lived another ten years, is buried just outside the City Park Cemetery in Nairobi. (Murumbi had expressed a wish that he be buried as close to his friend Pio Pinto as possible, but there was no room left in the cemetery.) In 2009, thanks to the efforts of Donovan and the Murumbi Trust, the graves became part of the Murumbi Peace Memorial, a garden containing sculptures by some of the artists Murumbi championed.

Donovan was also the person mainly responsible for stopping the export to Britain of some of Murumbi's papers and art that were part of the estate of Sheila Murumbi, who died without a will. Distant relatives of Sheila Murumbi were in the process of shipping the material out of the country when Donovan and others appealed successfully to the Government to halt further removals.

A substantial number of items associated with the Murumbis are on permanent display at the Nairobi Gallery, which is situated in a century-old colonial building in the heart of Nairobi. The Joseph Murumbi art collection occupies the ground floor of the National Archives, while Murumbi's stamp collection and papers are housed elsewhere in the building.

Donovan maintains a large collection of art and artefacts of his own at his African Heritage House outside Nairobi, which was built based on the mud architecture of Mali.

In his eulogy for Murumbi, William Ole Ntimama, at the time Minister for Local Government, praised Murumbi as 'an outstanding figure who was fired by neither political power nor personal ambition'. Murumbi, he said, 'always stood up for what he knew to be right. In this he never changed.' [98]

*The remains of the Murumbis' Intona home*

*The graves of Joseph and Sheila Murumbi, at the Murumbi Peace Memorial, City Park, Nairobi*

*Acknowledgements*

ACKNOWLEDGEMENTS

My thanks go first of all to Alan Donovan and Anne Thurston for their generosity in allowing the use of the material in *A Path Not Taken*. This material includes, in addition to Anne's interviews, further interviews Murumbi did with other people, including John Platter, and Alan's interview with Fitz de Souza. Alan also gave me access to a set of original transcripts of Anne Thurston's interviews which, among other things, contain details of Murumbi's stay in England not included in *A Path Not Taken*.

Thanks, too, to my early colleague Wendy Karmali and to all the people who gave of their time and insights. These include Pheroze Nowrojee, who graciously gave me a copy of the first chapters of a planned book on Murumbi that he and Sheila Murumbi collaborated on. Many thanks to Wolfson College at Cambridge University for providing me with a visiting fellowship in 2017 and to Professor John Lonsdale, emeritus professor at Trinity College, for serving as my advisor. The staff at the Kenya National Archives, in particular Richard Ambani, as well as the staffs of the archives of Churchill College at Cambridge, SOAS, the British National Archives at Kew, and Durham University's archives, were unfailingly helpful; so, too, were the librarians at Wolfson College and at the Centre of African Studies at Cambridge, and at the Schomburg Center for Research in Black Culture in New York. Several art experts, including Professor John

Mack of the University of East Anglia, helped me to gain at least a modest understand of the role of collecting and of museums in the Murumbi era. And thanks to the many authors of books and articles which helped to clarify the complexities of independence-era Kenya. Thanks also to Zahid Rajan for project management and publication, and to Zarina Patel for her careful editing of this book.

A few of the books I found most helpful were: *Kenya: A History Since Independence*, by Charles Hornsby; 'The Movement for Colonial Freedom, 1954-1964' a chapter in *Anticolonialism and the End of Empire*, by Stephen Howe; and *The Politics of Independent Kenya 1963-8*, by Cherry J Gertzel. Also helpful were various autobiographies and memoirs by Kenyans who played a role during the independence period, among them *Walking in Kenyatta Struggles* by Duncan Ndegwa, *Not Yet Uhuru*, by Oginga Odinga, and *So Rough a Wind* and *A Love Affair with the Sun* by Michael Blundell.

*A stamp from Murumbi's collection*

*About the Author*

ABOUT THE AUTHOR

Karen Rothmyer was an American Peace Corps volunteer in Kenya from 1966-68. After returning to America she pursued a career in journalism, working over the following decades for news organisations ranging from *The Wall Street Journal* to *The Nation* magazine, an American political weekly, where she was managing editor. She returned to Kenya in 2005 on a fellowship to teach journalism at the University of Nairobi, and spent most of the next ten years in the country, teaching and later serving as the first public editor of *The Star* newspaper. She now lives in the USA but makes regular trips to Kenya.

karen.rothmyer@gmail.com

## ENDNOTES

1 Fitz de Souza, in an August, 2014 interview with Alan Donovan included in *A Path Not Taken*, p 400.
2 Author's interview with Donovan, February, 2017
3 Cynthia Salvadori with Shaila Mauladad Fisher, *Settling in a Strange Land: Stories of Punjabi Muslim Pioneers in Kenya*, Park Road Mosque Trust, 2010, p 201.
4 Salvadori, op. cit, p. 202, footnote by Basheer Mauladad, content editor of the book.
5 Author's interview with Muriuki, February, 2017.
6 Charles Hornsby, *Kenya: A History Since Independence*, I B Tauris & Co., 2012, p 80.
7 A US Central Intelligence Agency biographic register entry for Murumbi refers to Murumbi and his wife as having had two sons. (Entry C06704500, 2 September 66, approved for release. 21 September, 2017.) Muthoni Likimani said she thought there might have been two children. I have found no further corroboration or information about the family.
8 Donovan's interview with De Souza.
9 Ibid.
10 Author's interview with Pereira, November, 2016.
11 Author's interview with Thurston, July, 2016.
12 Jabez T Sunderland, *India in Bondage*, Lewis Copeland Co. 1932, p xi in second edition.
13 Unitarian Universalist Association, http://uudb.org/articles/jabezsunderland.html, retrieved November, 2017.
14 Author's interview with Pereira.
15 W McGregor Ross, *Kenya from Within: A short political history*, Urwin Brothers Ltd., 1927, p. 41-42.
16 Ross, op. cit., p 55.
17 Ross, op. cit., p 430.
18 Malcolm MacDonald, notes on the eve of Kenyan independence, written in September 1963 and sent to the Secretary of State for Colonial Affairs and other officials, MacDonald Archive, Durham University 45 1-56.
19 Sir Frederick Jackson, *Early Days in East Africa*, Edward Arnold & Co., 1930, p 296.
20 Fenner Brockway, *Outside the Right*, George Allen & Unwin, 1963, p 103.
21 Brockway, op. cit., p 104.
22 Author's interview with Wheelock, October, 2016.
23 All foregoing in British National Archives, FCO 141/6887.
24 US CIA, Biographic Register, Joseph Anthony Zuzarte Murumbi, C06704501, approved for release 9 September, 2017.
25 Stephen Howe, chapter on 'The Movement for Colonial Freedom, 1954-1964', in Howe, *Anticolonialism in British Politics*, Oxford University Press, 1993, *passim*.
26 Minutes of the February 19, 1957 executive committee of the Movement for Colonial Freedom, in the MCF Archive in the SOAS Archives and Special Collections, MCF 01.
27 Kenya National Archives, MAC/MCF/159/2.
28 Author's interview with Munene, February, 2017.
29 Author's interview with Likimani, January, 2018.
30 Hornsby, op. cit., chapter *'Independence!' passim*.
31 Cyprian Fernandes, *Yesterday in Paradise*, Balboa Press, 2016, p. 118.
32 Author's interview with Kadhi, February, 2017.
33 Duncan Ndegwa, *Walking in Kenyatta Struggles*, Kenya Leadership Institute, second edition, 2011, p 464-465.

34 MacDonald notes of September, 1963, Durham archive, 45 1-56.
35 Letter from Murumbi to Kenyatta, February 13, 1963, Kenya National Archives, MAC/KEN/77/1.
36 *Africa Report* 01/06/63.
37 Author's interview with Muriuki.
38 Author's interview with Muriuki.
39 Ndegwa, op. cit. p 371.
40 Author's interview with Muriuki.
41 Author's interview with Munene .
42 Author's interview with Muriuki.
43 William Attwood, *The Reds and the Blacks*, Harper & Row, 1967, p 227.
44 Attwood, op. cit., p 256.
45 MacDonald letter to CW St J Chadwick, Commonwealth Relations Office, 30 June 1965, MacDonald Archive, 55/1/1-54.
46 Attwood, op. cit, p 264.
47 CIA biographic register, C06704500, approved for release 2 September, 1966.
48 Kenya National Archives, MAC/GTB/150/3.
49 Michael Hilton, master's thesis, '*Malcolm MacDonald, Jomo Kenyatta and the Preservation of British Interests in Commonwealth Africa*', 4th June, 2009, Trinity College, Cambridge, quoting MacDonald to CRO 23rd November, 1965, British National Archives, DO 207/42 f.9.
50 Hilton, op. cit., MacDonald note on talk with Njonjo, 29th May 1967, FRCO 36/124, f.32.
51 MacDonald telegram to Colonial Office, 25 May, 1967, MacDonald Archives, 54/5/59 1967.
52 Murumbi interview with the Afro-Asian News Service in New Delhi, September 13, 1963, in Kenya National Archives, MAC/KEN/84/8.
53 Letter of February 16, 1965 to N Krishnaswamy, Kenya National Archives, MAC/KEN/90/10.
54 Donald L Barnett and Karari Njama, *Mau Mau from Within: An Analysis of Kenya's Peasant Revolt*, Monthly Review Press, 1966, preface.
55 Ndegwa, op. cit., p. 370.
56 CIA biographic register, entry dated 21 May, 1965, C06704501, approved for release 21 September, 2017.
57 Undated telegram, Kenya National Archives,6 MAC/KEN/94/3.
58 Correspondence relating to Murumbi's resignation, Kenya National Archives, MAC/KEN/94/3.
59 Murumbi letter to Kenyatta December 31, 1966, Kenya National Archives, MAC/KEN/94/3.
60 'Murumbi Moves On' by Ngambi Kifaro in *Flamingo* magazine, Volume 2, number 2, Kenya National Archives MAC/KEN/87/8.
61 Interview with Ntimama in '*Makers of a Nation: Joseph Murumbi*', written and directed by Hilary Ng'weno, Nation Media Group, 2010.
62 Murumbi letter to Leslie Hale, January 1967 MAC/KEN/75/3.
63 Kenyatta letter to Murumbi dated September 23, 1966. Kenya National Archives, MAC/KEN/94/3.
64 Author's interview with Kadhi.
65 Author's interview with Donovan.
66 Author's interview with Nyairo, February, 2017.
67 Derek R Peterson, in Derek Peterson, Kodzo Gavua and Ciraz Rassool, editors, *The Politics of Heritage in Africa*, Cambridge University Press, 2015, p 4.
68 Peterson, op. cit., p 14.
69 Author's interview with Zetterstrom-Sharp, June, 2017.
70 CNN Marketplace Africa, by Jacopo Prisco, 18 January, 2016. http://www.cnn.com/style/article/africa-contemporary-art-investment/index.html, retrieved 21 November, 2017.
71 Author's interview with Nyairo.
72 Author's interview with Patel, February, 2017.
73 Author's interview with Nyairo.
74 Author's interview with Donovan.
75 Author's interview with Zetterstrom-Sharp.
76 *Daily Nation*, 2 May, 2003.
77 Kari Mutu, 'The Pioneer Artists of East Africa', in *The Star*, 1 April, 2015.
78 Karega-Munene, 'Origins and Development of Institutionalized Heritage Management in

Kenya' in Annie E Coombes, Lotte Hughes and Karega-Munene, *Managing Heritage, Making Peace: History and Identity in Contemporary Kenya*, I B Taurus, 2013, p 25.
79 Karega-Munene, op. cit., p 29.
80 Karega-Munene, op. cit., p 16.
81 Author's interview with Nyairo.
82 Author's interview with Muriuki.
83 Author's interview with Donovan.
84 Wendy Karmali interview with Donovan, 2016.
85 Author's interview with Donovan.
86 Karmali interview with Donovan.
87 Author's interview with Donovan.
88 Alan Donovan, *My Journey Through African Heritage*, Kenway publications, African Heritage Series, 2005, p 395.
90 Karmali interview with Donovan.
90 Author's interview with Muriuki.
91 Author's interview with Zahid Rajan, February, 2017.
92 Author's interview with Nyairo.
93 British National Archives, Kenya: archives, migration of records to the UK in 1963, FCO 31/3198.
94 Karmali interview with Donovan.
95 Karmali interview with Donovan.
96 Author's interview with Nowrojee, February, 2017.
97 *Daily Nation*, 18 March, 1992.
98 William ole Ntimama, eulogy, reproduced in *A Path Not Taken*, p 385.

# JOSEPH MURUMBI
*A LEGACY OF INTEGRITY*